Teaching Adults:
A beginner's guide for Christian leaders

by Colin Hurford

Second edition published in 2021 by Heddon Publishing.
Copyright © Colin Hurford 2021, all rights reserved.
No part of this book may be reproduced, adapted, stored in a retrieval system or transmitted by any means, electronic, photocopying, or otherwise without prior permission of the author.

The rights of Colin Hurford to be identified as the author of this work have been asserted in accordance with the Copyright, Designs and Patents Act 1988.

A CIP catalogue record for this book is available from the British Library.

ISBN 978-1-913166-42-7

Cover design and illustrations (apart from Chapter 11) by Maggie Humphry (www.maggie-humphry.co.uk)
© Maggie Humphry 2013

Book design and layout by
Heddon Publishing.

www.heddonpublishing.com
www.facebook.com/heddonpublishing
@PublishHeddon

Scripture quotations apart from Mark 4,35-41 are taken from
the HOLY BIBLE
NEW INTERNATIONAL VERSION
Copyright © 1973, 1978, 1984 by International Bible Society
Used by permission

The scripture quotation from Mark 4,35-41 is taken from the
New Revised Standard Version of the Bible, Anglicized
Edition copyright © 1989, 1995 by the Division of Christian
Education of the National Council of Churches of Christ in
the United States of America, and is used by permission. All
rights reserved.

The illustration and words following at the start of Chapter
11 are taken from the book *Human Relations in Modern Industry*
by R.F. Tredgold, published by Gerald Duckworth & Co. in
1963 then by Methuen & Co. Ltd. in 1965, and are
reproduced by kind permission of the family of Dr. Tredgold.

To my wife, Margaret,
And to Lawrence Chok Jin Tian
With grateful thanks for encouraging me to complete this book.
Also many thanks to Lawrence for his sponsorship and to my son, Terry, for his help with IT problems.

Thanks also to:
Maggie Humphry for the cover design and illustrations
Katharine Smith for her excellent work proofreading and preparing the book for publication
Graham Congdon and Bill Williamson - tutors in Adult Education

About the Author

The Revd. Colin Hurford has MA degrees in Theology (Oxford University) and Adult Education (Durham University), and a City and Guilds Certificate in Adult Education. He has been a Parish Priest for over 25 years and has spent ten years teaching, including seven years in Sabah, Malaysia, and eight months in Tanzania.

Colin writes: *The main characters in this book are fictitious and any resemblance to actual persons, living or dead, is purely coincidental. However, almost all the little stories illustrating different ideas are true, most of them based on my own experience. For example, I did have a spell put on me by a local medicine man (see Chapter 10) and, in a large gathering of Christians, the 82-year-old lady mentioned in chapter five did thank God aloud that there was always more to learn. The students' rebellion in chapter four is based, in part, on the class on Adult Education I attended. A number of the members grumbled about the way the tutor (an excellent teacher) was teaching, two or three threatening to give up the course.*

I do hope that this book will help many of those who have to lead small groups in their congregations, and will also encourage some to go a step further and obtain a formal qualification in Adult Education.

If you would like to contact Colin, he would be delighted to hear from you and happy to answer any questions relating to his book and his work.

You can email him at: colin.hurford@yahoo.co.uk

Contents

1. Introducing Theresa and Dominic 1
   Lessons to learn from this chapter *4*

2. Matthew, the tutor, and his students 5
   Lessons to learn from this chapter *10*

3. Planning a lesson 11
   Lessons to learn from this chapter *21*

4. Mini-teaching 22
   Lessons to learn from this chapter *32*

5. Solomon and the Bishop 33
   Lessons to learn from this chapter *36*

6. Different ways of teaching (Teaching Methods) 37
   Lessons to learn from this chapter *48*

7. Theresa's place 50
   Lessons to learn from this chapter *53*

8. Different ways of learning (Learning Styles) 54
   Lessons to learn from this chapter *64*

9. Teaching Aids 65
   Lessons to learn from this chapter *76*

10. Dominic has a problem with his group 77
    Lessons to learn from this chapter *85*

11. More about leading small groups 86
    Lessons to learn from this chapter *94*

Contents continued

12. Dominic and Theresa meet to plan their lesson 95
    Lessons to learn from this chapter *99*

13. A demonstration lesson by Dominic and Theresa 100
    Lessons to learn from this chapter *110*

14. Trouble at home for Nancy – different kinds of learning 111
    Lessons to learn from this chapter *122*

15. Matthew leads a meditation 123
    Lessons to learn from this chapter *128*

16. Changing peoples' attitudes (i.e. set ways of thinking) 129
    Lessons to learn from this chapter *141*

17. How to give a good lecture 142
    Lessons to learn from this chapter *157*

18. Assessing lessons and the progress of students 158
    Lessons to learn from this chapter *168*

19. Planning a course of lessons 170
    Lessons to learn from this chapter *185*

20. Demonstration lesson by Margaret and Ayung 186
    Lessons to learn from this chapter *197*

21. Demonstration lesson by Nancy and Solomon 198
    Lessons to learn from this chapter *208*

22. Party Time 209
    Lessons to learn from this chapter *217*

Contents continued

Appendices i
    Appendix A ii
    Appendix B iv
    Appendix C vii
    Appendix D viii
    Appendix E ix
    Appendix F xii
    Appendix G xiv
    Appendix H xvi
    Appendix I xviii
    Appendix J xx

Chapter 1

Introducing Theresa and Dominic

The bus slowly made its way up the hill towards the college. It was a very hot and humid day but the bus was only half full and Theresa had a window seat. She looked out at the big houses on the side of the road. Each had its own garden and some had swimming pools. Then she thought of the tiny flat where she lived with her six year old son, Joshua. The flat was part of a big block on the poor side of the city. It was hot and small but at least Theresa had her own kitchen and toilet - unlike the thousands of people who lived in one-roomed shacks just yards away from her home. Those people had to use dirty public toilets and they had to get their water from a single tap on a dusty pathway.

Theresa was, she thought, better off than many people she knew. But she couldn't help feeling jealous when she looked at the big houses. Most of them even had their own security guards! She thought again of the dusty slums, and the women she taught and tried to help. There were no police or security guards for them despite all the violence and crime.

The houses came to an end and she saw the walls of a big building coming into sight.

"That must be the college," she thought. She got up to make sure she would not miss the bus stop.

Suddenly, a motor cycle roared past the bus. A car horn sounded loudly. There was a squeal of brakes then the sound of a crash.

The bus stopped suddenly as the driver braked hard and Theresa was thrown forward. She tried to grab the edge of a seat but missed and felt herself falling.

"My face is going to hit the floor," she thought. Suddenly an arm shot out of the seat in front of her and caught her. For a moment, she could hardly breathe and then slowly she struggled upright.

"Are you alright?" she heard a voice say. She saw a good-looking African looking at her with a worried expression on his face.

"Thank you," she gasped. "I must get off here."

"Sit down a moment," said the African, "I don't think this bus is going to move just yet. Anyway, I'm getting off at the same stop so I'll make sure you don't get left behind."

Theresa collapsed into the seat and tried to recover her breath. Outside, a crowd had gathered. The driver of the car was looking angrily at his broken headlight. On the ground, in front of the bus, people were helping the motorcyclist to sit up. He was bleeding from a cut in his head and had grazes on his arm but he didn't look too badly hurt.

Theresa looked at the African. "Thank you again," she said, "you saved me from a nasty fall."

"No problem," he replied. "Where are you going?"

Theresa struggled in her handbag for a bit of paper.

"I'm going to the house of Dr. Matthew Mbwana," she said.

"I've got a class there."

"How strange," said the young man. "I'm going to the same place. Are you taking the course about teaching adults?"

Theresa nodded.

"Then we're going to be fellow students. Perhaps we should introduce ourselves. My name's Dominic."

"And I'm Theresa," she replied, quite pleased that she was going to see more of him. "Look, I'm feeling much better. Do you think we could get off the bus? There are plenty of people to help and I don't want to be late."

The two of them got off the bus and crossed the road, looking for the right house.

"This must be it," said Dominic, looking at a small but neatly painted bungalow. "Number 112."

Just then, another woman came up, also looking at a bit of white paper.

"Hello," she said. "I'm looking for Dr. Matthew's house."

"This is the place," said Dominic. "Are you going to his class as well?"

"Yes," she replied. "My name's Nancy Wong. What are your names?"

Theresa and Dominic introduced themselves then together they turned in at the gate of the house. The three of them, all teachers, were about to become students again.

Lessons to learn from this chapter

1. Each student is an individual with his or her own life, problems and work.

2. Some students will find it easy to study. Others, because of difficulties at home or at work, may find it much harder. For example, a student living in the shanty town near Theresa will have to spend a lot of energy simply to survive. This means that he or she may not have much energy left for studying.

Chapter 2

Matthew, the tutor, and his students

Matthew walked up and down his living room as he waited for his guests to arrive. He hadn't felt so nervous for years. He remembered how nervous he had felt when he first stood in front of a class of students as a newly appointed college lecturer. Now he was a senior lecturer at the Theological College. Most of the students he taught would become priests or ministers in churches or chapels. Matthew specialised in teaching Church History and the Old Testament.

But today he was starting something new. It was something he had never tried before. And he really wanted to make this new project a success. "Perhaps that is why I am feeling so nervous," he thought to himself. "I do want this course to succeed."

Matthew was starting a course on Adult Education. The title of his course was "How to teach adults."

It was a course he had been thinking about for a long time. He had discussed his ideas carefully with the college Principal. Between them they had decided to try an experiment. They had asked five different church groups each to send one student. These students would take part in an experimental course that Matthew had planned. Each student had to have some experience in teaching adults. In other words, they all had small classes of their own. But none of them had any training in how to teach adults. If the course was successful, it would become an important part of the college syllabus.

Matthew knew that much of the teaching at the college was not very satisfactory. Most of the lessons were actually lectures. The teacher talked and the students took notes. The students then tried to learn the notes and hoped they would be able to answer the questions set in the examinations. Some lecturers did work hard to make their lessons interesting. But many teachers gave the same old lessons year after year. Matthew knew that there were better and more exciting ways to teach adults. He wanted to pass this knowledge on.

As he waited for his students to arrive, Matthew looked at the room he had prepared. He had decided to hold the classes in his own house. The college was better- equipped for teaching but the classrooms were dark, with rows of battered desks. Matthew wanted his class to be much more informal. He knew his new students would be nervous and he wanted them to feel relaxed and at home.

There were six comfortable chairs arranged in a semicircle so each member of the group could see all the others. On each seat was a notebook and pen. At the front was an old blackboard on an easel. Matthew had carried these across from the college. The college had more modern equipment but Matthew thought that a blackboard was still the most useful help to teaching that there was. It was cheap and it was the one piece of equipment that all the students could get hold of for their own teaching. Matthew's wife had scolded him when he had struggled to get the blackboard through the door. "Don't you get chalk all over my mats," she had said. But she was only teasing him as she knew how much Matthew wanted the course to succeed. Even now she was in the kitchen preparing drinks for the guests.

Matthew went over in his mind what he knew about those who were coming. The most senior of the six students was Solomon. Solomon was a very experienced Anglican priest who worked with the Indian community in the city. He was married and had three grown up children. Matthew had heard rumours that one of Solomon's sons was in trouble. He thought it was something to do with drugs but he was not sure. Solomon had the reputation of being a very good, caring priest but was rather old-fashioned in his outlook. When he spoke at church meetings, he usually put forward traditional ideas. Solomon was training a group of people who would become ordained local ministers. They would become priests working at different churches in the city. For this work, Solomon was using a course prepared by the Archbishop's Board of Education.

The youngest student in the group was Dominic. Dominic was a twenty-two-year-old African who had been a Christian for only two years. He belonged to a local Pentecostal church. His church had given him the job of teaching the Christian faith to men who had been converted through one of the many missions the Pentecostal church held in the city. Dominic was a Primary School teacher but had no experience of teaching adult students.

The most interesting member of the group was Theresa. Matthew smiled to himself. He really shouldn't have any favourites, but Theresa was special. She was unmarried with a son about six years old. She came from one of the slums. When she became pregnant, her father, who came from South America, had ordered her to leave home. She had ended up trying to live in a cardboard shack on the edge of the city. Desperate for help, she had made contact with a local independent church and they had helped her through her pregnancy.

She had become a Christian and now she was employed by a local charity. She was paid a tiny salary to take literacy classes. Also, she trained small groups of women, many of whom were very poor. She taught them ways of improving their living conditions and helped them to fight for their rights. Theresa had great intelligence and charm - and a wicked sense of humour. "She'll liven up the group," thought Matthew.

The fourth member was Nancy Wong. She was Chinese and was forty-five years old. She had two sons, the younger still at college. Nancy was very much involved with evangelism. Because she was such a good evangelist, the Methodist church had chosen her to train church members to be evangelists. Matthew wished he knew more about her. It was important for the teacher to know the background of the students so he could plan lessons to suit them. But he would learn more as time went on.

Ayung was the fifth student. He was something of a mystery. All Matthew knew about him was that he was a Roman Catholic and that his Bishop had nominated him for the course. He came from one of the Islands and had made a long journey, by boat and by air, to get to the city. He was staying in a guesthouse run by the Catholic Cathedral.

Matthew again felt nervous as he thought of the sixth member of his group. She hadn't been nominated by anyone! She was a volunteer and a fellow teacher at the college. Her name was Margaret Ross. Margaret had been a Presbyterian Minister in the U.K. When she retired, she had offered to come and help at the college. Her specialist subject was the New Testament but she could teach other courses. She had been at the college for nearly two years and had become a good friend of Matthew and his family. When she heard of Matthew's plan she insisted she should join the course. She very much agreed with Matthew about teaching adults.

"It's no good just lecturing to our students," she said. "There must be better ways to teach. We have to get our students involved. They have so much experience and have a lot to contribute. Let me come to your course." Matthew had tried to persuade her to share the teaching with him but she had insisted on being a student.

Matthew liked Margaret very much but the thought of having such a senior teacher in his class dismayed him. Would he really be able to help a person like Margaret, a fellow lecturer, to teach?

Just then, Matthew noticed someone coming up his path. He went to the door and saw a tall man, probably in his thirties.

"Welcome!" he said, "Come in."

The man hesitated.

"Is this the right place for the training group?" he asked. "The taxi driver wanted to take me to the college but I told him it was at a private house."

"You're at the right place," answered Matthew. "Do come in. My name is Matthew."

"I am Ayung," replied the stranger.

"Ah," thought Matthew, "the mystery student." But before he had time to ask Ayung any questions, three more people came up his path, followed by Margaret. Then a small car, driven by a priest, turned into his drive and Matthew recognised Solomon. Matthew's students had arrived.

Lessons to learn from this chapter

1. Try to have a relaxed atmosphere in your class. Most students are nervous when starting something new. They need to feel welcomed. How the chairs are arranged is important. If your class is small, avoid rows of desks but with large classes this may not be possible. If you have to use desks, try to arrange them in a semicircle.

2. Learn as much as you can about your students and their backgrounds. This will help you to plan your lessons to suit your students. But respect their privacy. What you learn is confidential unless the student chooses to tell others.

3. Feeling a little nervous before starting to teach is a good thing as it helps to sharpen your lesson. Many famous actors feel nervous before going on stage and often clergy feel nervous before starting to preach. This is perfectly natural.

Chapter 3

Planning a lesson

Matthew welcomed his guests and served them with cold drinks. He was amused to see that the men had seated themselves on one side and the women on the other. It was time to start. He spoke to the group.

"As we are going to be working together for some time," he said, "it is important that we get to know each other. So I'm going to ask each of you to introduce yourselves. Tell us a little about yourself and also tell us about the classes you are teaching."

"Excuse me," interrupted Solomon, "but shouldn't we start with prayer?"

Matthew thought quickly. He must not cause Solomon to lose face, but at the same time he had to make it clear that he was in charge.

"Yes, I agree with you," he said, smiling. "But we can pray more effectively if we know each other's names. So we'll introduce ourselves, and then have a time of prayer. But first let me tell you something about myself."

Matthew introduced himself briefly, describing his job and family. He then spoke about his dream of starting a course at the college about how to teach adults. He told them how he hoped that the course he was starting now would provide the foundation for a college course.

Each of the others followed. Dominic was rather hesitant at first. He seemed a little overawed by the fact that he was one of the two youngest in the group. However, once he started describing his class and talking about how they had become Christians, he became much more confident. Theresa was pleased to hear that he wasn't married! Some of the things the others said were new to Matthew. He hadn't realised that Nancy, although a very good evangelist, had not persuaded her husband to become a Christian. Her husband was not hostile. He simply regarded Nancy's church work as her hobby.

Matthew also learnt something about the mystery man Ayung. Ayung was just thirty years old. He was married with two young children. He had been a teacher in a Catholic Secondary School but had left his job at the request of his Bishop. The Bishop had asked him to teach groups of people how to run their own churches. Ayung was also given the task of finding men and women to train as catechists. The other members of Matthew's group were all very interested as Ayung described how he travelled by boat from island to island, talking to Christians in the villages.

Ayung said he had been given one copy of a written course to use with the village people. But he was worried that he hadn't really enough knowledge to do the job properly. He thought his church should send a priest, but there were simply not enough priests to spare. Still, he felt God had called him to this task and he was going to try hard to succeed. It was clear to the others that both he and his family were making great sacrifices so that he could do this job.

After the introductions, Matthew asked Solomon to lead the group in prayer. He was pleased to see that Solomon had taken careful notes. This meant that Solomon was able to pray briefly for each person by name. He also prayed for God's help in the tasks each of them faced. Finally he asked God's blessing on the course. He said the prayers in a way which didn't allow anyone else to pray.

After Solomon's prayers, Matthew started his first lesson.

"During this course," he said, "we are going to cover quite a number of different aspects of adult education. We're going to think about questions like 'How do I plan lessons?', 'How do adults learn?', 'What helps adults to learn?' and 'What makes it hard for them to learn?' We are going to find out about different ways of teaching, and we will discuss how to lead small groups of people. I've got a sheet here which gives some of the different topics but I must point out that we may not follow the order printed on the sheet. I want to be fairly flexible. Also I want to give you time to ask questions or raise problems you would like us to think about."

Matthew handed out a rather grubby sheet of paper to each student. He had wanted to produce an attractive list with little diagrams to illustrate the headings. But the college computer had broken down again. So he had typed the list on his old-fashioned typewriter

How to teach adults

Main content of course

1. How do you plan lessons?
2. Different ways of teaching.
3. How do adults learn?
4. What helps adults to learn?
5. Helps to teaching, that is, 'Teaching Aids'.
6. Leading small groups.

7. Different kinds of learning.
8. What makes a good teacher.
9. Changing people's attitudes (set ways of thinking).
10. How to give a good lecture.
11. How to find out if your teaching is successful.
12. Planning a course of lessons.

He gave them a little time to study the sheet. "You may not understand all the headings but I hope they will become clear as we work through the course. Remember, if you want to add to that list or discuss anything different, please say so."

There was silence, so Matthew continued. "For this first lesson, I thought we would think about how to plan a lesson. Every time we teach, we should have a lesson plan. In other words, we should know exactly what we want to teach and how we are going to teach it."

Matthew paused for a moment, and then wrote on the board as he read out the heading:

PLANNING A LESSON

Dominic, Nancy and Ayung immediately picked up their notepads and pencils and waited for him to begin a lecture.

Matthew carried on, "You have all taught people, so you probably know how to make a plan. Dominic and Ayung, you will have been taught about lesson plans when you went to teacher training college. But then you were learning how to teach young people using textbooks. Teaching adults is different so, for the moment, forget what you have learnt. To begin with, I would like you to work in groups of two. Talk about the question 'How do I plan a lesson?' Then write down anything you can think of that is important in planning a lesson. It doesn't matter what order you write things down."

There was a rather uncomfortable pause, so Matthew had to make this a bit clearer. "You, Margaret and Solomon, you're sitting next to each other so you can easily make one pair.

Nancy and Theresa make another and that leaves Ayung and Dominic. Think of a lesson you have taught to your own little classes of adults. Then write down the different things that made up the lesson. For example, there must have been some kind of introduction so put down 'Introduction'. After that, write down the different parts of a lesson just as you think of them. I am giving you five minutes for this."

There was a bit more silence, but when Theresa and Nancy started chatting together, the others also started to talk. After five minutes all of them were talking quite loudly. Matthew stopped them and turned to his battered blackboard.

"Right," he said, "we'll go round the groups. Each group say one thing until we've put down everything you have suggested. Theresa, what's your first point?"

"Well, you said 'Introduction' so we put down 'Conclusion'," answered Theresa.

Everyone laughed.

"OK," said Matthew, "we'll put those down."

He wrote down 'Introduction' and 'Conclusion' on one side of the blackboard. "What else?"

"Verse of the Bible to memorise," said Dominic.

"Aim," suggested Margaret, and others continued with 'Talk', 'Lecture', 'Exercise' (this was from Ayung the schoolmaster), 'Homework', 'Discussion' and 'Action to take'. These last two were from Theresa.

"Now," said Matthew, "let's put your suggestions into some sort of order. I am going to start with the aim of the lesson. All parts of the lesson depend on what you are aiming to teach. 'Talk' and 'Lecture' are nearly the same so I will put those down together."

Matthew built up a list from their suggestions.

Aim
Introduction
Talk/Lecture

Discussion
Exercise
Verse to memorise
Conclusion
Homework/Action to take

"Now that really is an excellent start. You've put together the outlines of a lesson plan. Notice again that I put 'Aim' right at the beginning. Margaret, you said 'Aim'. What exactly did you mean?"

"The aim is the main thing you want to teach in your lesson," replied Margaret. "It may be just one thing or it could be two things. I don't think I should have more than two aims otherwise I will confuse my students."

"Can you give an example?" asked Ayung.

"Yes. Some time ago, I was teaching a lesson about the prophet Amos. Amos, as you probably know, is one of the books in the Old Testament. My lesson was the first lesson of four so I just had one aim. This was: 'To help the students discover from the book of the prophet Amos some of the bad things that were happening in Israel at the time the prophet was writing.' My whole lesson was centred on that aim."

"What were the bad things?" asked Theresa.

"That's another issue," said Solomon.

"But I want to know," said Theresa, "I come across a lot of bad things in my work."

"Things like how the rich oppressed the poor. How girls served as temple prostitutes. How the traders had altered their scales so they gave lighter measures than they showed. These and a lot more are referred to in the book of Amos," answered Margaret.

Solomon was clearly impatient. He could see they were getting off the main point which was describing an 'Aim'. But Matthew let Theresa have just one more word.

"You know, I've never read Amos before," she said. "Perhaps I should try it."

"I think it would help you with your group," said Matthew. "The prophet Amos is very clear that God is on the side of the poor. But now let's get back to our lesson planning. The 'aim' is what you really want to teach your students in that lesson. And it is very important. It needs just one or two sentences, but put it down right at the start. It will help you to keep to the point."

"The next thing I have put down is 'Introduction'. Why do you think that a good introduction is so very important?"

"I suppose because you want to make your students pay attention," replied Nancy. "You don't want them to go to sleep."

"That's right," said Matthew. "Think carefully about your introduction. See if you can make your group really interested in what you are trying to teach them."

Theresa spoke again. "Margaret, how did you introduce your lesson about Amos?"

"I asked the students if any of them had been cheated at any time in their lives," replied Margaret. "That led to a heated discussion. Then I said, 'Let's see how people were cheated in the time of Amos.' They were all eager to find out!"

"Thank you," said Matthew. "Now, let's go on with our list. After the 'introduction' comes 'talk' or 'lecture'. That is the main part of the lesson. But it needn't be a talk. It could be a discussion, or some other activity. There are different ways of teaching that you can use for the main part of your lesson. We will think about that later in the course. So I will write down, 'Main part of teaching'.

Going on from the main part of your teaching, do you need all these four things in every lesson: 'Verse to memorise', 'Conclusion', 'Homework', 'Action to take'?"

They thought for a bit and then Theresa answered, "I suppose you just need 'Conclusion'. The conclusion can be different for different lessons."

"That's right," answered Matthew. "So we can simplify the plan. But remember the conclusion or ending must strengthen and sum up what you have been trying to teach. Another word that would do instead of 'conclusion' is 'consolidation'. So far as teaching is concerned, to 'consolidate' means to 'make strong or more solid' something you have already taught. You help people to remember what you have taught in the lesson. The conclusion could be an 'activity' as Theresa suggested. Or it could be Dominic's 'verse to remember'. It could be Ayung's 'exercise'. It depends on the lesson. So I am going to simplify the lesson plan to just four headings:

Aim
Introduction
Main part of teaching
Conclusion/consolidation

I'll just give you a couple of minutes to jot those two tables down."

Matthew paused while, for the first time, his students took down notes of what he had taught them.

"Now, I'm going to 'conclude' or 'consolidate' this lesson by giving you an exercise. This is a bit of homework, something for you to prepare for the next time. At the next lesson, I want you all to do what I call a 'mini-teaching' session. I want each of you to prepare a lesson which lasts just fifteen minutes. Then I want you to teach your lesson. It can be on any topic you choose.

"Also, I want you to write down your lesson plan, just a simple plan, and bring it with you so we can look at it. Have you any questions about that?"

"You mean that you want us to stand up in front of this group and teach a lesson?" asked Nancy.

"I'd be too scared," said Dominic.

"No you wouldn't," replied Margaret. "You're among friends and we will all be interested in what you have to teach us."

"Can it be a lesson we will actually teach to our own group of students?" asked Solomon.

"Of course," Matthew answered, "or you can use a lesson you have already taught, except you will have to shorten it. You can ask us to pretend to be members of your own little groups if you like."

"It's going to be hard to stick to fifteen minutes," said Nancy.

"That's part of the exercise," replied Matthew. "But I'm sure you can do it. Because you will all be doing some teaching, the next lesson will be longer than usual. Is that alright with everyone?"

No one objected, so Matthew continued. "Now to end this lesson, I am giving you a copy of my lesson plan for you to look at. It is more detailed than just the four points we've listed but don't worry about that. Also, because it is the first lesson of the course, it is a little different from a normal lesson plan. We had to introduce ourselves and I had to tell you about the course. So there are three 'aims' rather than one."

Dominic looked a bit bewildered. "No teacher has ever shown me how he was teaching before. I always thought a college teacher just lectured and the students took notes."

"Many teachers do just that," said Matthew. "Lectures can be good ways of teaching people, but there are many other ways as well."

They all studied Matthew's lesson plan. Then Nancy spoke out. "You've put down times - ten minutes, thirty minutes and so on - for each part of the lesson. Do you have to keep to those times?"

"No," replied Matthew. "The times are just a guide to make sure you don't spend too much time on any one part of your lesson. Also, if you've got a fixed length for your lesson, putting down times for each section helps to make sure you don't go on too long. Your students may have to get home and don't want to be late."

"You've got an extra heading to the four we wrote down," said Theresa. "You've put in 'Objectives'. What does that mean?"

"I didn't try to introduce 'Objectives' to you in this lesson," replied Matthew. "When I was studying how to teach adults, it took me a long time to understand the difference between 'Aims' and 'Objectives'. Briefly, an 'Objective' describes something that you want your students to be able to 'do' as a result of your lesson. So my 'Objective' for this lesson is that you are able to plan a simple lesson based on the four headings we have written down. It is something you can actually do and which can be tested. I hope this will become clearer as we learn more.

"Some lessons may not have any objectives. Others will. For example, if you are teaching people how to read a lesson in a church or other place of worship, a good objective would be to 'make sure the reader can be heard clearly'. That is something you can test. Does that help to answer your question, Theresa?"

"Yes," replied Theresa, "I suppose when I teach my literacy classes, a good objective for one lesson would be that people can write their own names."

"That's right," replied Matthew. "But you don't have to have objectives for every lesson. Don't worry about 'Objectives' for the moment. Just make sure you have a clear 'Aim'. Now, does anyone want to stay for coffee?"

Three decided they would stay but Mathew noticed that Solomon went out without saying very much at all. "Oh dear!" thought Matthew, "I think I have upset him."

Lessons to learn from this chapter

1. Members of the group or class need to get to know each other. If the group is small, the members can introduce themselves. If it is a large group, try dividing people into smaller groups so they get to know at least some of their fellow students.

2. It is important to pray at each lesson both for each other and for the lessons but when the students have got to know each other, let them decide how they would like to organise the prayers.

3. Planning a lesson. A simple lesson plan is:
    Aim
    Introduction
    Main part of lesson
    Conclusion

Think very carefully about the aim - so your lesson keeps to the points you want people to learn.

Think carefully about your introduction so that you get the attention of your class or group.

4. Note that in this lesson, Matthew's conclusion is to give the students an exercise. He asks them to prepare and then teach a mini-lesson. This exercise 'consolidates' what they have just learnt.

5. Many lesson plans include the word 'Objectives'. An objective describes something that you want your students to be able to do as a result of your lesson - something that can be tested. Not all lessons need to have objectives but all must have clear aims.

NOTE: For Matthew's lesson plan, see Appendix A at the end of the book.

Chapter 4

Mini-teaching

The next week, the six students met again at Matthew's house. They were nervous at the thought of having to give a lesson in front of everyone else. Before they began, Matthew asked them what they would like to do about praying together. This led to an enthusiastic discussion and they decided that they would have a time of prayer at the end of each session.

Ayung said that if they wanted to pray for each other properly, they needed at least ten minutes. The others agreed. Dominic and Nancy suggested that everyone should be given a chance to pray if they wanted to. Solomon wisely pointed out that any prayers that were said should not be talked about outside the group. Confidentiality was very important. The discussion took quite a long time because everyone was keen to avoid the next item on the programme – the mini teaching! However, Matthew ruthlessly cut them short.

"Time to move on," he said. "I hope you've prepared your

fifteen minute teaching sessions?"

They all nodded.

"Good," he said. "We'll draw lots to see who goes first. I've got your names here."

Matthew put folded slips of paper into a battered old hat and asked Solomon to draw the names. He raised a laugh by drawing out his own name first. Then came Dominic, followed by Ayung, Theresa and Margaret, with Nancy coming last.

Matthew was watching them carefully. He saw that while Solomon and Margaret seemed confident, Nancy and Ayung were quite worried, while Dominic looked very scared. Matthew decided that some encouragement was needed.

"How are you feeling?" he asked the group.

"Frightened," said Nancy.

"I don't think I'm going to be any good at this," said Dominic. "Can I leave it until I've learnt a bit more?"

"No way," replied Matthew. "But there's no need to be so worried. I'm quite sure your lesson will be very interesting. Everyone is bound to be a bit nervous but remember this is not a test. The most important thing is that we encourage and support each other. So even if you are feeling nervous, don't worry about it. We are all friends and we will all learn something from each other.

"Now, as you listen to each lesson, I want you to write down two good things about it. That is, write down two points you find helpful. Make two positive comments. Then I want you to write down just one thing you think could be improved - just one criticism. Even if you think the lesson is hopeless, which I am sure you won't, I only want one criticism. Remember again that people learn best when they are encouraged. Have you any questions?"

Nobody replied.

"Right," said Matthew, "the one condition is that the lesson should only last fifteen minutes. I've got an alarm clock here!"

Matthew produced a battered, old-fashioned alarm clock. "I'm going to set it for fifteen minutes and then it will go off.

If the person has not finished, we will allow two more minutes to end the lesson. Then we will spend just five minutes commenting on the lesson. Will you start, Solomon?"

Matthew listened very carefully to all six of the presentations. He ignored his own instructions to the class, making notes of all the strengths and weaknesses of each person. These notes would help him to judge the progress of each student. They would also help him to work out how he should plan lessons. Matthew made a list of topics his students had chosen.

Solomon: The meaning of Christ's death. Solomon gave his lesson the title 'The Atonement'.

Dominic: Why Christians should read the Bible every day.

Ayung: The need for local people to take an active part in running their own church.

Theresa: Theresa asked the group to imagine that an open sewer was running past their houses. Then she asked them to work out what they could do about it.

Margaret: The writer of St. Mark's Gospel. What kind of person was he?

Nancy: Talking to people about Jesus.

All the students gave interesting introductions to their lessons. But all except Theresa and Margaret followed their introductions by giving straight talks.

Solomon started off with a story about a priest, Maximilian Kolbe, who, during the Second World War, volunteered to take the place of someone who was going to be killed. Then he gave a lecture about how Jesus had atoned for our sins.

Dominic was very nervous and spoke too quickly. But he impressed the group with his sincerity and enthusiasm. He captured their attention by describing his own conversion and how the New Testament had helped him to know Jesus more clearly.

Ayung's lesson started off in a very interesting way. He told a story about a sick person in one of the villages, who wanted to see the parish priest. The nearest priest was in the big town a long way from the village. By the time the priest arrived at the village, the person had died. There were just not enough priests to go round. But after his introduction, he just gave a talk about how the Bishop's Committee had discussed the problem. The Committee decided that each village should have its own team of people. These people would be trained to help in situations like that.

Theresa started by giving a description of the dirty stream running past the houses and children playing in the water. She then led a discussion in which she invited each person to put forward suggestions about how to tackle the problem. To end her lesson, she asked the group to vote on the best course of action.

Margaret started her lesson by saying she wanted to introduce the group to a friend.

"This is difficult," she said, "as my friend is dead! My friend is St. Mark, the writer of the third Gospel. I feel he has become a friend because of what I have learnt about him by studying his Gospel."

Margaret then gave each member of the group a Bible with pages already marked to save time. She asked them to look up verses, in St. Mark's Gospel and the Acts of the Apostles. From these verses, she built up a picture of what St. Mark might have been like as a person and why he wrote his Gospel.

Nancy made her lesson interesting by telling a story about a person whose life had been changed by an evangelist. But then, like most of the others, she gave a lecture, about what an evangelist should do. She did, however, make the others laugh by telling about a woman who had tried to evangelise in the wrong way. An angry husband had almost thrown the woman out of the house because she told him he would go to hell if he didn't listen!

After each student had given the mini-lesson, Matthew asked for their comments. They had clearly taken to heart the message about encouragement. All agreed that the introductions to the lessons were interesting and had got their attention.

For the second good point, there were a number of different comments. They thought Solomon and Ayung spoke very clearly. They were impressed by both Dominic's and Theresa's enthusiasm. They thought Nancy had some good points to make, especially about not putting people off. But the lesson that seemed to have really impressed them was Margaret's.

"We found out things for ourselves," said Dominic.

Margaret had given an excellent lesson. She encouraged the students to think about the writer of St. Mark's Gospel as a person. She told them that Mark had written in the old Greek language. She then showed them, by reading from a literal translation of the Greek, that Mark was not very good at writing Greek grammar. And she helped the group to discover for themselves that Mark had little confidence in himself.

However, her lesson upset Nancy and, to some extent, Ayung. They had never thought of Mark as a human being like themselves. They had been taught to think that St. Mark, when he wrote his Gospel, had simply written down words put into his head by God.

Theresa, however, was fascinated by the lesson. She was deeply moved when Margaret suggested that Mark probably lived among poor people and was not a good Greek scholar. Yet he had written one of the most important books in the world!

Theresa thought of the little groups she taught in the slums.

All the women were desperately poor. She wondered if these women could do something really worthwhile. It couldn't be as much as Mark. His Gospel had helped millions and millions of Christians. But perhaps, with God's help, she and her friends could do something about the terrible conditions they lived in. Maybe they really could make a difference.

Matthew then asked them to point out one bad thing in each lesson. No one would make a start! So Matthew pointed out that people could not improve until they knew their weak points. This led to some criticism about ways of speaking.

"He spoke too quickly," said Nancy about Dominic.

Ayung's comment was, "I thought Nancy needed to vary the way she spoke. It was all the same tone of voice."

"There was too much about the Bishop and his committee," said Margaret about Ayung's lesson.

Theresa did criticise Margaret's lesson but very mildly.

"The trouble is," said Theresa, "that in my group only half the women can read. So I couldn't ask them to look at verses in the Bible. It would be too hard for them."

It was obvious that Solomon's lesson was far too hard for all of them except Margaret. But only Theresa said this clearly.

Her actual words were, "I enjoyed the introduction, but when you started talking about 'atonement', 'substitution' and 'redeeming', I couldn't understand any of it. But I did remember that atonement meant at-one-ment. Jesus died to make us one with God."

Solomon was angry despite Theresa's last comment. He criticised Theresa's lesson by saying that sewers had nothing to do with Christianity! Nancy, to Matthew's surprise, agreed.

"There's going to be trouble here," thought Matthew. He felt he had to be very careful in his summing up.

"Thank you very much for these lessons," he said. "So much hard work has gone into them. I've learnt quite a bit from them myself. But how many of you have heard things that are puzzling and challenging? How many of you have heard things you disagree with or can't understand?"

Four of them put their hands up.

"Right," continued Matthew, "I want you to think about what that means for you as a teacher. As you teach other people, there are going to be many times when you will say things that will be too hard for your students to understand. You will often teach people new ideas which they cannot accept at first. They will feel like you feel now; puzzled or confused. Perhaps they will feel a bit angry. So try to think how your students will feel when you teach them something that is new or hard to understand."

Ayung said, "We had an experience of that in our village. One of my friends is an agricultural teacher. He goes round to villages trying to teach the farmers better ways of growing crops. But the people in the village would not take any notice. That didn't mean they were stupid. They were just frightened of trying new things. And they were worried that the new methods might not work and they would be short of food. So my friend said, 'Just try it my way with a small part of your field and see if the results are different next harvest.' Some of them did and were surprised to find that the Agricultural Officer was right. They did get better crops by following his way."

"That's a good example," said Matthew. "New knowledge is sometimes hard to take in. Some of you found that, especially with Margaret's lesson."

Matthew realised it was time to bring the lesson to an end so he continued,

"We've had two classes now. Is there anything you would like to say about the lessons? Is there anything you would like me to explain or anything you don't understand? Have the lessons been helpful?"

There was a silence and then Dominic burst out, "When are you going to start teaching us? When are you going to give us proper lessons?"

"Yes," said Nancy "I was wondering that. I mean, it's been quite interesting, but we haven't started to learn anything yet."

There was a gasp of surprise from the others. They had not

heard a student criticising a teacher openly like that. Matthew felt himself becoming angry.

"It is never easy," he thought, "to take criticism even when you expect it. But I asked them the question so I can't complain if I get a straight and honest answer."

"Can you explain a bit more about what you mean when you say you haven't learnt anything?" he asked.

"We have learnt something," said Dominic. "And it's been interesting. But you haven't given us any notes. We could learn a lot more if you gave us a lecture and we took notes. How do we pass the examination if we don't have notes to learn?"

"I'm sorry," said Matthew, "I thought you knew that there is no examination."

"But what is the point of taking a course if you don't have an examination and a certificate to say you have passed?" asked Dominic.

"At the end of the course, you will all, I hope, get a certificate," said Matthew. "But having an examination is only one way of passing a course. We will be talking about other ways of testing students in a few weeks' time. But thank you for your question, Dominic. I will think about what you have said and talk more about it next time. It is too big a question to answer quickly. And I would like you all to think about Dominic's question too. But perhaps it would help if you try to answer a rather different question. You can write it down if you like."

They all took up their notebooks and pens. This was what they were more used to!

"This is the question," continued Matthew, looking at his class, "Do you learn more:
1. By listening to someone talking
2. by looking at a picture
   or
3. by doing something?
Now, let's pray for each other."

The prayers this time were a bit subdued but Ayung did pray

for Theresa and her many problems trying to help the poor. Nancy prayed for Margaret that she might not be led away from the true faith by too much study!

As they left, Solomon shook Matthew's hand and thanked him. He said he would be in touch! "Does that mean he is not coming back?" thought Matthew.

Margaret stayed behind for a moment. "They were a bit hard on you, weren't they?" she said. "I think I'd have been more upset than you if they had spoken to me like that."

"I must admit I was upset when Nancy said they hadn't learnt anything!" said Matthew. "But I was expecting them to rebel. I am introducing new ideas very quickly. Perhaps it's a good thing this happened so soon. It brings out into the open what they are feeling."

"You mean, you planned for this to happen?"

"Well, shall we say, I was hoping it would. I know it is hard when your students criticise you. But which would you prefer? Would you like a group of students to just sit and listen to what you say and then speak badly about you when they are on the way home? Or would you like a group that's willing to speak out about what they feel?"

"Oh, the second without any doubt," answered Margaret. "I want a group of students who are willing to think for themselves and who are not afraid of expressing opinions."

"So do I," Matthew replied. "But the trouble is that almost everything in our educational system encourages them to sit there and say nothing - and hope they will pass an examination at the end. This is not right, especially when it comes to teaching adults. I am worried about Solomon, though. I am not sure he will come back."

"Well," said Margaret, "I'll just have to say a prayer for him. Even though he is a bit traditional, he's too good to lose."

Meanwhile, the other students were on their way to their homes thinking very different thoughts.

Solomon was driving away from the class still feeling very angry. What right had that woman to tell him his lesson was too hard to understand? She shouldn't be in the class if she couldn't understand. A woman criticising him! He would make an urgent appointment to see the Bishop and ask to be released from this course. It was all just a waste of time. The tutor, Matthew, wasn't even teaching properly anyway.

Dominic also left the meeting with mixed feelings. He had to give a report to his church the next evening. He hadn't understood all that Margaret had said about St. Mark's Gospel. But he knew that if he said anything about that particular mini-lesson, the church leaders would stop him going. They were very strict and taught that God had inspired every word of the Bible. The idea that the writers of the Bible, and especially the Gospel writer Mark, might be a man like other men would be thought of as dangerous teaching.

"But I am enjoying the course," thought Dominic. "And I'd like to get to know Theresa better. If I leave the class, I might not see her again. I think I will just give a general report. I will say it is interesting and helpful but it is too early to judge how good the course is. That would be perfectly true."

Dominic went off to his little house feeling much more cheerful.

Lessons to learn from this chapter

1. Students, especially adult students, are very nervous and frightened of getting things wrong or being criticised. Treat them gently!

2. Lecturing students is often not the best way of teaching unless you have a large class. Take great care to make your lecture interesting if you do use that method of teaching. There are some suggestions in Chapter 17.

3. When you introduce new ideas to your students make sure they begin to understand them before going on to the next lesson.

4. The more you get to know your students' abilities, the better. You can plan your lessons more effectively.

5. Don't be afraid of disagreement but make sure it is brought out into the open. Then try to find a solution. Sometimes teachers and students must agree to have different opinions.

NOTE: See Appendix B for a summary of the mini-teaching lesson plans.

Chapter 5

Solomon and the Bishop

The following week, Solomon drove slowly to the class. He had seen the Bishop but his talk had not gone as he expected. When Solomon told the Bishop that he didn't think the course would be of any help to him, the Bishop had looked embarrassed.

"But I would very much like you continue with the course," the Bishop said. "Solomon, you know the group of students you are helping to train for the ministry?"

"Yes," Solomon replied.

"Well, some of them have been complaining that they cannot understand your lessons. And two told me that, while they had a tremendous respect for you as a parish priest, you were a rather boring teacher!"

Solomon was very upset. He was almost rude to the Bishop.

"Well, if that's what they think, perhaps you had better get someone else to take the group."

"No! No!" said the Bishop. "I want you to take the group. You are one of my best Parish priests. You know more about running a parish and caring for people than most priests in my Diocese. You have a deep love for Jesus Christ and you have a lot to give to these students. All you need to do is learn a little more about how to teach adults. I know you've visited schools and taught children. But, apart from the usual Confirmation classes, you haven't had a great deal of experience of teaching adults. I want you to learn a new skill."

"But I am too old to learn now," retorted Solomon.

"Let me tell you a story," answered the Bishop. "Some years ago, I was at a conference of Christian leaders. There were about one hundred and fifty people at the conference. We had a time of prayer. During that time, the leader asked us to thank God for something He had done for us recently.

"One of the members of the conference was a lady doctor who had worked in China and other countries. She had seen more human suffering and had more experience of God's power, including miracles, than most of us. She was eighty-two years old and we all respected her very much. And her prayer was, 'Thank you, Father, that no matter how old we are, there is always something new to learn.' We all felt very humble that this devoted Christian, even at her great age, could look forward to learning new things.

"So, Solomon, I want you to continue with the course. I want you to learn as much as you can about teaching adults. At the end of it, come and tell me what you think. If you think the course is no good, I will take your word for it. But I feel you have much to give to these students of yours. It is just a case of finding the right way to teach them. Will you complete the course?"

Solomon had great respect for his Bishop. In any case, a parish priest can hardly say 'no' to his Bishop! Rather reluctantly he agreed to do what the Bishop asked. "But," he thought, "I will take careful notes of all that happens. At the end, the Bishop will know whether the course is worthwhile."

"Alright," he said to the Bishop, "I'll do that."

"Good," said the Bishop. "Now, how's your family?"

"Very well," replied Solomon. And then he realised why he had been feeling so sad and why he had been getting angry with people.

"No," he went on. "That's not really true. All are doing well except Thomas, our youngest son. He left home when he was eighteen and we haven't heard from him for three months. I've been asking friends in the city if they have seen him but all I have heard is that he might be taking drugs. His two brothers have also searched for him. My wife and I are very worried but we feel so helpless. There's nothing we can do."

"Why did he leave?" asked the Bishop.

"Oh, the usual family arguments about the kind of friends he was seeing. He got involved with some bad characters and I spoke to him about it. But he wouldn't listen. The next thing we knew was that he had packed a bag and left. He did leave a note for us saying he would be in touch. He's not a bad young man at heart. But we haven't heard anything."

The Bishop talked with Solomon for some time. He ended by telling Solomon that he would pray for Thomas every day until Solomon had some news. Then he blessed Solomon and his family. Solomon left feeling a little better about his problem. He felt very thankful that his Bishop was so understanding. He almost forgot that he had gone to see the Bishop about leaving the course!

Lessons to learn from this chapter

1. No matter how old we are, there is always more to learn. Learning is for life!

2. Each student will have his or her own personal cares and may be facing problems. These problems could affect the way he or she speaks to others or behaves in the class. Be sympathetic.

Chapter 6

Different ways of teaching (Teaching Methods)

Matthew had thought very hard about this next lesson. He had discussed the problem with his wife, Ruth. He often found that talking to Ruth about things helped him to come to the right decision. She had a gift for helping him to see a problem more clearly.

"I'm trying to introduce new ways of teaching to these students," he told her. "But they think I am not teaching them properly. I am worried that if I don't give them more traditional teaching they will think the lessons are a waste of time and stop coming."

"How many think you are not teaching them properly?" Ruth asked.

"Four out of the six," he replied. "Margaret and Theresa understand what I am trying to do. But the others are worried. I think they are frightened of new ideas. The new ways of teaching are very strange to them."

"I thought that the whole point of the course was to introduce them to new ideas," said Ruth. "Surely, if you go back to the traditional way, it will be more difficult to teach them new ways. I know it's hard for them but you should stick to your plan."

"I think you're right," said Matthew. "I will just change the beginning and the end of the lesson. If I can show them at the end of the lesson that they really have learnt a lot of things, they will be much happier. Say a little prayer for me."

"Of course," said his wife. "But I'm sure it will work out alright."

Matthew felt much better as his students began to arrive. They, however, looked a bit uneasy. "They are embarrassed after Dominic's question last week," thought Matthew. "I'll have to put them at ease and help them to relax."

Instead of getting straight down to the lesson, he spent a little time greeting them and chatting. He served them with drinks together with little titbits Ruth had prepared. As the students talked to each other, they became more relaxed. Matthew timed this carefully as he had a very concentrated lesson to get through. So before any of the students became impatient, he asked them to be seated for the session.

"Last week," he began, "Dominic was worried that I was not teaching you properly. He raised a very important point and most of you agreed with him. He thought I ought to be giving you some straight teaching so you could be making notes. But remember that, in this course, I am trying to show you new ways of teaching. So at the end of this lesson, I want you to do two things. When you each gave a short lesson, you wrote down two good points about the lesson and one bad point. Now it is my turn to be judged. During my lesson today, I want you to note two good things about the lesson. Then I want you to write down two bad things, two criticisms. Maybe something in the lesson was too hard for you. Maybe there was something you didn't agree with. Is that clear?"

"Yes," said Theresa and Ayung together.

"O.K." said Matthew. "Today, we are going to look at different ways of teaching. 'Ways of teaching' are called 'Teaching Methods' and there are about twenty different kinds. Twenty is too many to think about in one lesson so I'm going to consider eight or ten. It will depend on how much time we have."

He wrote on the board,

DIFFERENT WAYS OF TEACHING
OR different <u>Teaching Methods</u>

Matthew continued, "After we have thought about this, I am going to give you some reasons why a teacher should use different ways of teaching. You can take notes if you like, but I will give you a summary on a sheet of paper at the end of the lesson."

There was a general murmur of agreement and Nancy, Solomon and Dominic all got their pens and writing pads ready.

"To begin with," said Matthew, "I want you to write down as many different ways of teaching as you can think of. Some of them have already been used in the last two lessons, including the mini-teaching that each of you gave."

"Here we go again," thought Solomon. "He's asking us to do the work. Why can't he just tell us and write them on the board instead of wasting time?"

Under the heading 'Criticisms', Solomon made a note on his pad, "not teaching clearly about methods." But, as he made his criticism, the words of the Bishop came back to him, "Cooperate and see what you can learn." Solomon changed his mind and started to think seriously about Matthew's question, 'How many different ways of teaching can I think of?' He started to make notes.

Dominic was struggling. He simply didn't understand the question. What did Matthew mean by 'different ways of teaching'? He looked around. Theresa, Solomon and Margaret were scribbling away. He started to panic. What would the others think if he hadn't written anything down? They'd think he was a dull student and despise him! A vivid picture came to him of when he was in the classroom as a teenager. The teacher had made fun of him because he couldn't answer a question. Now, his mind had gone blank in exactly the same way. He couldn't think of anything at all!

Matthew was watching carefully and noticed that three of his students were struggling and needed help.

He interrupted, "Just let me explain the question a bit more. Dominic, when you asked last time why I didn't teach you and let you take notes, you were thinking about a particular way of teaching. The teacher stands in front of the class and talks, while the students take notes. That is called 'lecturing'. It is a way of teaching that has been used for centuries and is still an important way. Most of you used that method when you gave your mini-lesson. So you can write down, 'Lecturing'."

Matthew wrote 'Lecturing' on the blackboard, underneath his headings.

"Now, can we think of other ways? Can you remember the main part of Theresa's lesson? Did she give a talk?"

"No," said Dominic remembering this clearly. "She had a discussion."

"Exactly right," said Matthew. "And 'Discussion' is another way of teaching people. You can learn a great deal from discussion. But there is an important fact about discussions. The leader of the group must make sure that those taking part in the discussion do keep to the point."

"You did that in the first lesson we had," said Theresa. "I wanted to talk about the Book of Amos, but you were teaching us about planning a lesson."

"Yes," said Matthew, "I had to draw the group back to the main aim of the lesson. But it was quite alright to have a short time answering your question as the question was clearly very important to you."

Nancy had been listening closely. "When you made us form groups of two and asked us to think about planning a lesson, is that another way?"

"Yes," said Matthew. "Working in small groups is a good way of teaching, especially if the students look as if they are going to sleep! Get them into small groups; two, three or four people. Ask them to talk to each other and they wake up. It's called 'raising energy levels'. You may remember that, after a short time, you all started talking quite excitedly."

Matthew wrote 'Working in small groups'. "Now, can you think of any other methods?"

Nancy answered, "Solomon told us a story at the beginning of his lesson. I thought that might be another method."

"Excellent," replied Matthew. "Story telling is one of the most powerful methods of all. Have you thought that Jesus, one of the greatest teachers of all time, told many stories? It's a wonderful teaching method. Now can you think of any other teaching methods? Ayung, you've got a list there."

Ayung had been taught different teaching methods when he had been trained as a secondary school teacher, but he was only just beginning to realise that he could apply some of these to adult teaching as well.

"These were not used in the teaching sessions, but I've used them in my own teaching," he said. "I've got 'Demonstration', 'Exercises' and 'Solving Problems'. I used demonstrations in science lessons. It would be better if the students could do the experiments themselves, but we don't have the apparatus so I did experiments in front of the students. And in Mathematics, I often used the other two methods. I gave the students exercises to do and problems to solve."

"That is really good, because you can use all those methods when teaching adults." Matthew added these three to the list. "Have any of you put down other methods?"

"Brainstorming and role play," said Margaret.

"Excuse me," asked Nancy, "but what do you mean by those?"

"Well, 'brainstorming' is simply asking a class to shout out any ideas that come into their heads about a particular question or problem. We did that when Matthew, at the start of the course, asked the little groups of two to shout out different parts of lesson plans. Matthew just jotted down everything anyone suggested then put them in the right order. I often use that method when I am planning a sermon. First I write down everything that comes into my head. Then I sort out the ideas and decide which are important."

"What do you mean by 'role play'?" asked Solomon.

"Role play is quite different," continued Margaret. "We use that method when we are training students to go visiting. Suppose you want to teach them how to visit the sick. You get one student to pretend he is a sick person in hospital and then two or three others pretend they are visitors. They act out the parts and then the rest of the class comment on what they say and do. You can learn a great deal about right and wrong ways of visiting by using that method."

"I could use that when teaching people evangelism," said Nancy. "Someone could pretend to be a non-Christian and someone else a Christian. It would be a good way of teaching."

Matthew completed the list on the board:

Teaching Methods
Lecturing
Discussion
Story telling
Small groups
Demonstration
Exercises
Brainstorming
Role play

"We've got eight different methods," said Dominic excitedly, "and I couldn't think of one to start with! I must have been stupid."

"Not at all," said Matthew. "It was just that you didn't know what I meant by 'ways of teaching'. And that was my fault for not explaining it a bit more clearly. Has anyone got any more methods?"

Solomon, despite his earlier opposition, had actually found he was quite interested. He rather tentatively put forward his ideas.

"We do take our students on visits to other Parishes to see what they can learn from different churches," he said. "I suppose you could call that a way of teaching. And sometimes we use a practical example in teaching pastoral work. For example, I make up a story of someone coming to my office with a family problem. I ask the students to think how they would help that person. I don't use true stories because often people's problems are confidential. The students seem to enjoy those kinds of lessons more than the ordinary lessons."

"You've put your finger on two very powerful teaching methods," said Matthew. "Going to a different Parish or visiting a place where the students can learn more, for example a school or a prison, is called a 'field trip'. As long as you can do it without much expense, it can be very helpful. Looking at a typical pastoral situation, a family in trouble or something similar would be called a 'case study'. People learn a great deal from this teaching method. So we can add these to our list."

Matthew wrote down these two suggestions.

"That makes ten altogether. I think that's enough for this lesson. Have you any questions so far?" He paused for a moment. "Alright, we'll go on. Before we finish, we need to think about one more question. The question is, 'Why should we use different methods of teaching?' In other words, why can't we stick to the good old-fashioned method of giving a lecture?"

Matthew turned the blackboard round and wrote on the clean side:

WHY USE DIFFERENT METHODS?

He continued, "I think you've had enough discussion, so I am going to give you some straight teaching. This is not really a lecture because I am going to keep it quite short. The name for the kind of teaching I am going to use now is 'oral teaching', which simply means 'giving a talk.' Don't hesitate to interrupt with questions if there is anything you don't understand. I am going to give you five reasons for using different teaching methods and these are:

One: It keeps the interest of the students. The lessons do not become boring and learning is more fun.
Two: We can learn from each other. Adults already know a great deal and can help each other to learn. Sometimes the teacher can learn as well.
Three: Different kinds of learning need different methods. For example, if you want to learn to drive a car, it's no good going to a lecture and hearing a teacher tell you how to drive. You've got to get into the car and do it.
Four: People learn in different ways. If you always use the same way of teaching, people who learn better from another way of teaching will suffer. They will not do as well as they should. We will learn more about this in the next lesson, so don't ask questions about this point just now.
Five: I'm going to write this down, as it is very important. Don't worry if you haven't taken notes. The sheet I am going to give you at the end of the lesson has the list of teaching methods on it."

"Do you remember," Matthew asked, "the question I asked you to think about at the last lesson?"

"Yes," said Nancy. "It was, 'Do you learn more by listening, seeing or doing?'"

"I think people would learn more by actually doing something," Ayung suggested.

"That's quite right," answered Matthew. "Experiments

have been done with students and the results are quite surprising."

He wrote on the board:

People remember   **20% of what they hear**
40% of what they see
80% of what they do

"So," continued Matthew, "if you give a lecture, the students will remember about one fifth of what you have said. If you show them a picture and discuss it with them, they will remember nearly half of what they see. If the students actually do something themselves, they will remember more than three quarters of what they do. This, as I have said, is a very important principle of learning. So do make sure you use different teaching methods. Well, I think that is enough for today. We've covered a huge amount of ground for one session. Now, at the start of the lesson, I asked for your comments. I asked you to tell me two good things about the lesson and two bad things. Let's start with the bad news. What are your criticisms?"

There was a rather uncomfortable silence. None wanted to be the first to criticise.

Matthew broke the silence, "Dominic, you had a serious criticism to start with."

"Well," said Dominic, "It was that I just didn't understand your question about different ways of teaching, but I do now."

"Right," said Matthew. "I should not have put you in that position because if a person doesn't understand, he panics and doesn't enjoy the lesson. If one of your students loses face in a lesson or finds it too hard then he or she won't come back and probably won't go to any other classes either! So that's a very valid criticism. Any other bad points?"

Ayung answered, "I think, perhaps, we have had too much to learn in this session. I don't think I can remember it all."

"You're probably right," said Matthew. "That is why I am

giving you a summary sheet which you can take away. Also all the points will come up again later in the series. But if you can't back up your lesson with a set of notes - these are called 'handouts' - it would be better to cut down the amount of teaching in a lesson. For example, I could have introduced only five teaching methods this lesson and then five more next time. So don't give your students headaches by making them learn too much at once. Are there any other criticisms?"

"Excuse me," said Solomon, "but you do move about the room an awful lot when you are teaching. And you wave your arms about. It's quite distracting."

Matthew laughed.

"I know I do," he said. "I try to remember to keep still, but I forget. I'm sorry for distracting you. Perhaps I should sit down more next time. But you've raised an important point. Most of us have some fault in the way we teach, which is part of our nature. We must find out what this is and try to stop doing it all the time. Thank you for reminding me. Are there any other criticisms?"

No one spoke.

"You're very kind," said Matthew. "Now let's look at the good points."

Solomon very graciously answered, "I have learnt quite a lot of new things. I hadn't realised how many different ways of teaching there are. And I understand the need to vary the teaching so pupils don't get bored."

Theresa said, "I agree. I think my teaching will change as a result of what I have learnt today. I'm going to try and work out a different kind of lesson for my next group."

"What I have found interesting," said Margaret, "is that most of what we have learnt, we already knew inside ourselves. It's as though much of the knowledge is already there. It just needs to be drawn out and put in order."

"Thank you, Margaret," said Matthew. "I firmly believe that is true when teaching adults. Of course, some of the things you teach have got to be new things. You are the teacher and you know more about your subject than your pupil. That is your special expertise. But your students, if they are adults, have a great deal of experience of life. And in many subjects, they already know a lot of things. Often they don't realise this. I do think an important part of the teacher's job is to draw out of the students knowledge they already have. So how do you feel about this lesson, Dominic?"

"I feel good. I think I have learnt a lot of things," Dominic replied.

"It's helped me too," said Nancy.

Matthew was quite relieved. "Well, thank you all," he said. "Here is the sheet I promised. In the next lesson, we are going to learn about what makes a good teacher. I will also talk about different ways of learning.

"There is a small bit of homework for the next session. I want you to think of your time at school and at college, if you went to college.

"What kind of lessons really excited you and helped you to learn? What kind of lessons turned you off or perhaps made you think you were a failure? Now we just have enough time for our prayers before we go."

Later that evening, Ruth asked Matthew how his lesson had gone.

"Very well," said Matthew. "I'm glad I stuck to my plans. Even Solomon seemed to be satisfied. I think he will stay the course now."

"You see," said Ruth, "I told you not to worry."

Lessons to learn from this chapter

Matthew's handout:
1. Different teaching methods:
    Giving a lecture
    Having a discussion (Note: the leader of the group must make sure those discussing keep to the point)
    Telling a story
    Dividing students into small groups
    Giving a demonstration
    Giving an exercise
    Brainstorming
    Role play
    Field trip
    Case study

2. You use different teaching methods because:

    (a) It makes your lesson more interesting.
    (b) It fits in with what you are trying to teach; different kinds of learning need different ways of teaching.
    (c) Students can learn from each other.
    (d) People learn in different ways. For example, a person who does not learn easily from a lecture will learn more from a different way of teaching.
    (e) Students remember:
    20% of what they hear
    40% of what they see
    80% of what they do.

Other points to remember (this is not part of Matthew's handout):

1. Watch carefully to see if any of your students are finding things too hard.

2. Don't be afraid of changing your teaching method (as Matthew did when he saw   Dominic was struggling.) Be flexible.

3. Here is a list of some other teaching methods you could use:

(a) Brains Trust - bring in two or three experts to answer questions from students.

(b) Gaming - get students to play a game which focuses on a particular subject or problem. Christian Aid and other organisations produce such games.

(c) Team teaching. Two or more people work out a lesson together and learn a great deal themselves as they do this. (See chapters 13, 20 and 21.)

(d) Workshops. Plan a day for the group to spend together working at different projects in turn. These take a great deal of organisation but can be very helpful when teaching a large class as the students can be divided into small groups.

(e) Tutorial – teaching-one-to one. Helpful to do at least once with each   student to review their work and give them a chance to ask questions they do not want to discuss with the whole group. Not possible with a large class.

(f) Drama. People can learn a great deal watching short plays.

NOTE: See Appendix C for Matthew's lesson plan.

Chapter 7

Theresa's place

Dominic and Theresa got on the bus going to the city centre.

"You're very quiet," said Theresa.

"I still feel guilty about speaking to Matthew as I did," said Dominic. "I really learnt a lot from that lesson but just a week ago I was criticising him. It was a very rude thing to do."

"No, it wasn't," said Theresa. "Matthew asked if we had any questions, and you did. I think he was actually pleased you said what you did. Some of the others were thinking the same thing so it was good for you to ask the question. Don't worry about it."

They talked a bit more about Matthew's lesson and Dominic asked Theresa about her work in the shantytown.

"Can I come to one of your classes?" he asked.

"Well, a number of my groups are for women only," answered Theresa. "But I've got a literacy class tomorrow that's open to men and women. You can come to that as an observer. It's held in the True Jesus Church."

"I'd like to do that," said Dominic. He thought he would find the class interesting. Actually he was more interested in seeing Theresa again!

Theresa gave him instructions about how to find the church. By then the bus had reached her stop so she said goodbye.

The next evening, Dominic followed Theresa's directions carefully and walked through narrow streets. He found the church and went in. Theresa was already there and welcomed him. She introduced him to a group of women and some young men; almost boys, really. She explained to her students that he was a friend interested in literacy classes and told the students to take no notice of him as he would just be an observer. After a short time she began her class.

Dominic was very interested to see that she was using pictures for her lessons. She pointed out objects in the pictures, for example 'boy'. She wrote down the word 'boy' and asked them to copy it. Then she made short sentences to describe what the boy was doing. The students all had exercise books and pencils and painstakingly wrote down the words. Dominic noticed that some of them had difficulty in forming the letters but Theresa went very slowly. Then she went around the class checking their work. She gave the quicker students extra work while she helped the slower ones. After the lesson, Theresa invited Dominic back to her flat for a drink.

Dominic walked with her along dirt paths, past houses built of corrugated iron. The smell was pretty bad.

"Is this the sewer you were talking about?" he asked.

"Yes," replied Theresa. "We are going on a protest march to the council offices next Monday to try and get the council to do something about it. We don't have any money to bribe the officials. I think that if we keep putting pressure on them, they will get so fed up of us that they will do something. The trouble is that people who live in these shacks just don't count.

But we've got a newspaper on our side and the editor is sending reporters."

"It's a good idea to keep on and on about a problem," said Dominic. "It's called 'pestering'. There is a story in St. Luke's Gospel about a poor widow who pestered the judge so much that after a time he decided to hear her case."

"I know the story," said Theresa, "but I'd never thought of it applying to what we are trying to do. So, like that widow, I will go on pestering. But here is the entrance to my flat. We have to go up four flights of steps."

Together they climbed up the smelly steps with graffiti on the walls.

"This is it," said Theresa, opening the door.

Inside was a living room with a tiny kitchen and a door which Dominic thought must lead to a bedroom and a toilet. There was a woman and a small boy there. The boy ran up to Theresa and put his arms round her.

"This is Benedict, my son," Theresa said. "And this is Maria. She looks after Benedict when I am teaching."

"Hello Maria," said Dominic, "Hello Benedict. How old are you?"

Benedict turned away and hid behind his mother.

"He's six years old, aren't you, Benedict? He's a bit shy at first but he'll talk to you when he gets used to you."

Theresa went to the kitchen and prepared some drinks for the four of them. Benedict produced a little wooden car and showed it to Dominic. The two of them soon started talking. Dominic was used to dealing with young children.

Time seemed to pass very quickly and Dominic was reluctant to leave. He sensed Theresa felt the same, but he had to get back to his church to prepare for the service next Sunday.

"I'm sorry, I must go," he said. "Perhaps I can come again. Or maybe you can come to my house."

"Yes, come again!" said Benedict.

"You've made a hit there," said Theresa, "you'll have to

come. Benedict will pester me until you do."

Dominic said goodbye to the three of them and set off along the dusty paths. It was getting dark and he felt horrified that Theresa had to walk along such paths. Gangs of youths were standing at street corners and it seemed a dangerous place to be in. Soon, however, he found the main road and went off to his own church.

"Five days," he thought, "before I can see her again. I'll have to find some way of meeting her more often!"

Lessons to learn from this chapter

1. Remember that your students have other work to do. They also have cares at home. This may mean that they haven't much time or energy for studying.

2. Persevere with what you feel is right. And remember the parable of the widow and the judge in Luke 18, 1-8.

Chapter 8

Different ways of learning (Learning Styles)

When the students arrived at Matthew's house for the next lesson, they got quite a shock. The comfortable chairs had all been pushed to the walls and there were two rows of three desks with the blackboard in front.

Matthew came into the room and moved straight to the blackboard. He didn't offer them drinks but began his lesson immediately.

"Good evening," he said. "We have a great deal to learn in this lesson so I will start straight away. Would you please sit down."

Dominic, looking puzzled, didn't know whether to sit at one of the desks, or in a more comfortable chair at the side of the room. Solomon, however, immediately chose one of the desks and the others followed his example.

"I'm going to talk about different learning styles," said Matthew. "You can take notes if you like."

The students got out their notepads and pens as Matthew started his lecture. He wrote the heading on the blackboard.

DIFFERENT WAYS OF LEARNING
(Learning Styles)

He spoke in a rather dull voice, without much expression. He pointed out that people learn in different ways. Experiments had been carried out in England and America to try and identify these ways. He went on and on, still speaking in a dull tone, talking about four different learning styles. Then he started to talk about 'activists' and 'theorists'.

As he went on talking, Theresa felt more and more upset. She couldn't understand a word he was saying! She looked around at the other students. Solomon was taking notes. Nancy had started taking notes but had given up. Ayung and Dominic just looked as if they were going to sleep.

"I can't stand this anymore," she thought. "I just hate this kind of teaching. It's just like we had at school. I'll have to go out."

She was just about to get up when she saw that Margaret was smiling. Then Matthew wrote the words 'Field Dependent' on the board and Margaret started to laugh.

"Matthew, I think we've had enough," she said.

"OK," said Matthew, in a more normal voice. "I agree. Let's have a break. Will you help me to move these desks and put the chairs back in place?"

"I don't understand," said Solomon. "Aren't you going to finish the lecture?"

"I'll explain in a moment," said Matthew. "First, let's have a drink."

They moved the desks and chairs to the side and arranged the more comfortable seats in the usual semi-circle. Matthew's wife came in with a tray of orange drinks. When they had all sat down and were sipping their drinks, Matthew went on.

"How did you feel when I was lecturing?" he asked.

"I nearly walked out," said Theresa. "I just felt I was back at school. I hated school. The lessons were boring and I couldn't understand them. I spent most of my time either staring out of the window or trying to attract the attention of the boys."

She paused and looked at Matthew. "You did all that on purpose, didn't you? You wanted us to feel that way?"

"Not quite," said Matthew. "I didn't know what you would feel. But I asked you last week to think of good and bad times at school. I was trying to put you back into your school classroom. I wanted to help you remember what you felt like. But what do the others think?"

Nancy spoke. "It reminded me of some the lessons I had. I couldn't understand quite a lot of what the teacher was saying. When I did ask one teacher to explain, he looked at me as though I was stupid. All the other girls laughed at me. So I didn't ask any more questions. I was frightened the others would think I was a dull student."

"Some of my teachers were like that," said Ayung. "We just took notes and then learnt them. And if we didn't understand, we kept quiet. But we had some good teachers as well."

"We'll think about the good teachers in a moment," said Matthew. "What did you feel, Solomon?"

"I found the first part quite interesting but I did not understand what was meant by 'field dependent'. Have any experiments been done in our country about different learning styles?"

"Only one that I know of," said Matthew, "but how did you feel about the way I was teaching?"

"I enjoy listening to lectures," replied Solomon. "But I thought the way you spoke was - well, boring. Did you intend to speak in such a dull way?"

"Yes," said Matthew. "That was part of the demonstration. There are a few teachers who speak like that."

"Margaret," said Theresa, "what did you feel? I noticed you were smiling and then started to laugh."

"I know Matthew very well. I soon realised what he was trying to do," said Margaret to the others. "I knew he wouldn't go on lecturing for a long time so I didn't take it too seriously. But when he got to the 'field dependent' bit, I thought it was time for him to stop. When I was a student at college, there was a lecturer who taught exactly like that. It reminded me very clearly of him. In fact, I almost felt I was in his classroom even though it was over forty years ago. Dominic, what did you think?"

"I had to leave school at Primary Six," said Dominic, "and the lessons in primary school were quite interesting. But later, when I went to college, two of my teachers spoke like that.

"Other teachers taught in an interesting way and one was very good indeed. I always paid attention when she was teaching us. And I learnt a lot from her when she gave lessons in local primary schools. We had to observe her teaching as part of the course."

"Thank you, Dominic," said Matthew, "I'm glad you had some good teachers. We'll come back to them in a moment. But now, what makes a bad teacher?"

"Giving a dull lesson that's hard to understand," said Theresa.

"Not answering questions and making fun of students when they do ask," said Nancy.

"Not taking an interest in the students," said Ayung.

"Good," said Matthew, "so what does a bad teacher make you feel?"

"He makes you feel you want to leave school," answered Dominic.

"So," continued Matthew, "if you are a bad teacher, what will the students in your own classes feel?"

"They'll probably leave the class," said Theresa.

"Will they go to any more classes after that?" asked Matthew.

"Probably not," said Nancy. "In fact, I suppose you could say that if you teach badly, you might stop a person from learning anything at all!"

"Yes," said Matthew. "A bad teacher can put you off learning for the rest of your life. That is a very important principle. But just think how the way I taught you at the beginning of this lesson brought back memories of school or college. Margaret said it brought back memories of forty years ago. You will find that most of your students still have very vivid memories of what it was like at school. Some memories will be good, some bad. And if you bring back bad memories, students will get discouraged and stop coming to lessons."

"But not all teachers are like that. You will all have had good teachers and I am sure you will be good teachers yourselves. So let's look at the good side. What lessons did you enjoy at school?"

"I had a very good Mathematics teacher," said Ayung. "I really enjoyed Mathematics. That's why I became a Maths teacher myself."

"In what ways was he a good teacher?" Matthew asked him.

"He always explained things carefully and made sure everyone understood, even students who found Mathematics difficult. Sometimes he would tell little stories to keep our attention. And he would come around the class to look at our work. If we were struggling, he never told us off but explained the question again. And he would ask if anyone had similar problems. He encouraged us and never made us feel that we were dull students."

"Let me make a list of the things that make a good teacher," said Matthew.

He turned to the blackboard.

WHAT MAKES A GOOD TEACHER?
Explaining things carefully
Giving encouragement

Making lessons interesting

"Any other headings I can put down?" asked Matthew.

"Showing the students how to do things," said Nancy. "I was really interested in Home Science because the teacher gave good demonstrations that were easy to follow. Also she explained the reasons for doing things as she went along so we learnt the theory as well. Dominic, you told us about a very good teacher who could demonstrate how to teach children. In a way, it was the same with my Home Science teacher."

"I think," said Margaret, "that the two most important things are, first, being really interested in your subject. Enthusiasm is the word I would use. And, second, being interested in your students and caring for them."

"That's right," said Ayung. "When I think about it, the thing that really made me want to teach Mathematics was the enthusiasm of my teacher. He was a good teacher, as I said. But he really enjoyed Mathematics."

"I will write those things down," said Matthew, and he added to his list on the board:

Good demonstrations
Enthusiasm for what you are teaching
Caring about your students

"Theresa," asked Margaret, "were there no lessons you enjoyed?"

"There were a few," said Theresa. "Sometimes our English teacher would organise a play or a discussion. I liked taking part in those. And I enjoyed the Art lessons in secondary school. I was good at drawing. But we stopped Art lessons after the second year because the school had to spend more time preparing us to pass exams. The examinations were the important things. But I never passed any."

"Thank you, Theresa," said Matthew. "I will write one more thing down."

Developing the gifts or talents of a student

Matthew continued, "In this part of my lesson, I have asked you to work out what makes a good or bad teacher. In our discussion, Theresa raised one of the most important points in education and I want you to think very carefully about this. It may mean changing the way you think about learning. You see, in most countries, schools are mainly teaching pupils to pass examinations. Pupils have to learn facts and take notes. Then when the examination comes, they have to write out as much as they can remember of what they have learnt. If they are good at learning in this way, they get good marks and pass. If they are bad at taking notes, or if they cannot remember things well, they get bad marks and fail. Then they are called poor students.

"But a lot of people simply are not good at learning in this way. They learn better through other ways - drama, debating, doing things, planning things.

"You, Solomon, are obviously very good at learning by listening to lectures and taking notes. But you, Theresa, are not good at that kind of learning."

"I know," said Theresa, "I have always been a failure."

"No! No!" Matthew almost shouted. "You are not a failure. Just because you do not learn well through the traditional teaching methods, it does not mean you are a failure. It simply means that you learn better in other ways. For example, how much have you learnt by going to Government departments and bullying them into taking action for poor people?"

"A tremendous amount," said Theresa. "I've learnt about dealing with people, about budgets, about the bureaucracy. I've learnt where I can get help for projects. I've learnt all kinds of things. But that won't help me to pass examinations."

"And I'm sure you've learnt a lot through teaching people," continued Matthew. "You've learnt a lot by helping them to write and sign their names. And that is real learning. It is just as good as studying from books. You, Theresa, learn better by 'doing' rather than by 'studying'. Have you been to any lectures since you took up your present post?"

"Only one," said Theresa, "but I could have taught the lecturer quite a lot. He was right in some things, but he didn't know much about the real conditions people live in."

"There you are. You are a very good learner but your method of learning is different from Solomon's. And," Matthew said very strongly, "it's not a poorer way of learning. It's as good a way of learning as any other way. Let me give an example. Think of a good carpenter. He learns how to be a good carpenter by actually making things. He has to learn some theory as well but making chairs and tables is the most important way of learning. And remember, Jesus was a carpenter. There is a lovely picture of Joseph teaching the boy Jesus how to smooth wood. And it's even more amazing when you think that Jesus was God. Joseph taught God how to make a stool or a yoke for an animal. That's an amazing thought! But let me get back to the subject."

The others were fascinated by Matthew. They had never seen him so passionate. He went on, "You see, much of our education makes us believe that there is only one way of learning - that is studying books, taking notes and passing examinations. Ever since we were children, we have been taught to think that way. So we think the only true kind of education is passing examinations. And we think that if we don't do well in school, and if we don't get good marks, then we must be dull students. That way of thinking is wrong.

"You are not a dull student, Theresa, you are a very clever person. It's simply that you learn better by doing things rather than by sitting at a desk and studying. Remember what I said about learning to drive a car or a wagon? It's no good sitting at a desk and learning the theory. You've got to get into the car and drive it."

Matthew went on, "In adult education, this is a most important fact. Many adults have no confidence in themselves because they think they are dull students. You, as teachers, must put that confidence back into them."

"Does that mean the traditional way of teaching is all wrong then?" asked Ayung.

"No, not all wrong," replied Matthew. "There are many good things in the traditional way. And with large numbers in classrooms, lecturing and setting examinations is probably the only way. But lecturing can fail many students. Those students will learn more if the teacher uses different ways of teaching. This is because people learn in different ways. And different ways of learning are called 'learning styles'.

"There's been quite a lot of research in the Western countries, especially England and America, about different learning styles. But very little research has been done in other countries. There's some research to show that Africans probably learn better in groups rather than on their own. Africans are very community-minded so it's a fairly obvious conclusion. The term used in education for those who learn best in groups is 'field dependent' but you needn't bother to remember that."

"But can we do anything to help people who learn in different ways?" asked Dominic.

"Of course you can," said Matthew. "Just look at the list I've put on the blackboard. You can take an interest in your students. You can encourage them and not criticise them too much. You can make your lessons interesting. And, very important, you can use different teaching methods. Make sure you use different ways of teaching. Some of your students will learn better using the traditional way, through straight teaching and notes. Use that way but not too often. Some will learn better through discussion and argument. Some will learn better by actually going out and doing the job and then coming back and discussing how it went. Some will learn better by planning things. Study your students and make sure you help them as individuals. Above all, don't let them feel they are bad students. You can put them off learning for ever if you do that."

"Does that mean we should never use lectures when we are teaching?" asked Solomon.

"No, it does not mean that," replied Matthew. "Everyone can learn from an interesting, well-planned lecture. But make sure that in your lecture you give examples and tell stories. This keeps students interested. We'll discuss more about how to make lectures interesting later in the course. But if you use that teaching method every time, those who are not good at learning from lectures will soon fall behind. We can learn from every kind of teaching method. But we get more from a lesson that fits in with our particular way of learning."

"I'm confused," said Nancy. "I thought teaching was such a simple thing. The teacher stood in front of the class and taught. If the students didn't learn, they were bad students. Now you're saying that if the students don't learn, it's the teacher's fault!"

"That is mainly true when you are teaching adults," said Matthew. "Of course, there are some lazy students. They won't learn much whatever way you teach. There are some students who enrol for the wrong kind of course. That kind of student needs help to find a course that is suitable. But most adults who have the courage to come to classes really do want to learn. So the teacher has to make sure he teaches in such a way that all the students can learn.

"I think that you, Nancy, Theresa, Dominic, Ayung, have shown considerable courage in coming to this class. It can't have been easy for you. And you, Solomon, have shown courage in coming even though I have used different methods from the ones you are used to. So congratulations to you all for persevering!"

Matthew started to pass some handouts around the group.

"I think I've talked too much," he said. "We have done enough for today so here is a sheet which summarises this lesson. Next week we'll look at another important reason why we should use different teaching methods. Now who is going to lead our prayers tonight?"

Lessons to learn from this chapter

Here is Matthew's handout.

1. A bad teacher:
Gives boring lessons
Has a dull way of speaking
Does not answer pupils' questions
Makes fun of students who ask simple questions
Does not take an interest in the students

2. A good teacher:
Gives interesting lessons
Explains things carefully
Answers students' questions even if they are simple ones
Is enthusiastic about his/her subject
Cares for students
Uses different ways of teaching

3. People learn in different ways. 'Ways of learning' are called 'Learning Styles'.
Some learn better by listening to talks or lectures
Some by doing things
Some by discussion and argument
Some by planning courses of action
Some by solving problems

4. A good teacher plans the lessons in such a way that all the students can learn. He uses different teaching methods so that students with different learning styles will find things in his lessons that are particularly helpful to their way of learning.

Remember: A bad teacher can put people off learning - sometimes for the whole of their lives. A good teacher encourages people to continue learning.

Chapter 9

Teaching Aids

"I wonder what we will find this time," said Nancy to Theresa as they walked through Matthew's gate. "Last time it was those desks. Do you think he has another surprise for us?"

"We'll soon see," answered Theresa as they knocked on the door.

"Do come in," said Matthew, opening the door. "There's no need to wait."

They walked into the living room. "I told you there would be something different," said Nancy. "Look at that!"

There was a laptop computer with a projector showing pictures and illustrations on a white screen. A television was on one side. At the back were various pieces of equipment. Theresa recognised a flipchart, a CD player, a smartphone, and a video camera on a tripod. She had never handled a video camera but had seen them in shop windows. There was one thing she had not seen before.

"What's that?" she said, pointing to a box-like object.

"That's an overhead projector – called an 'O.H.P.' for short," answered Matthew. He switched it on and a white light shone on the screen at the front.

"You can write on this sheet," he said, holding up a transparent piece of plastic. The O.H.P. will project what you write on the screen. Theresa, write your name on this sheet."

He offered Theresa a marker pen.

She wrote her name on the sheet and Matthew put it on the glass at the base of the O.H.P. Theresa's name showed on the screen.

"You can use this for charts and diagrams which you can prepare beforehand," continued Matthew.

"That's a useful piece of equipment," said Dominic, who had just come in. "Our lecturers use one occasionally but it's too expensive for me to use in my group. I have to make do with the flipchart."

"I use a flipchart," said Theresa, pointing to the stand with pieces of paper hanging from it. "I get a very small allowance to buy things that help with my teaching, but even buying paper is quite expensive. You can write what you want on each sheet using a large coloured pen and then just flip the sheet over to see the next one. It's useful when you are preparing a lesson but when I ask for suggestions from my group, I use a blackboard. It would take too much paper if I used the flipchart."

"Some of these teaching aids are quite expensive," said Matthew. "The smartphone is mine. You can get a projector to show pictures or short videos from your phone, but the cheap ones are not very good. I have borrowed the laptop, projector and video camera from the college. Let's spend a bit of time seeing how these things work."

Matthew switched on the television and went to the video camera. He pressed some buttons. Soon they were all laughing as the television showed them as they were coming into the room and they could hear themselves speaking to each other.

"You can take pictures with this and show the pictures on the television set," said Matthew. "We use it to show the students what they look like and how they sound when they are preaching or taking services. You remember, Solomon, you said I moved around a lot when I was teaching. Well, the students took a picture of me walking up and down all the time I was teaching. It was most embarrassing."

"If you have a smartphone," said Solomon, "you can get a friend to take a short video of yourself. It's not as good as recording a whole sermon, but it does give you an idea of how other people see you. We use a laptop with a very good projector in our church, to project the words of hymns and prayers onto a large screen. We used to use supplementary hymn books, and hymns typed on bits of paper. The projector saves us a lot of time. We can also use it to project pictures to illustrate sermons or lessons, but we have to be careful about copyright. However, you need to have someone who has good computer skills. It's easy to make mistakes if you are not very good at using computers."

"Another problem connected with using this kind of equipment," said Matthew, "apart from some pictures being copyrighted as Solomon has said, is that you can find an enormous amount of information on the internet. You can spend literally hours searching for helpful articles and pictures. If you do use a laptop or computer, make sure you plan your lesson very carefully so you know exactly what will help you to teach your lesson. For example, if I was teaching a lesson on the temptations of Jesus I could use pictures like these which I have copied from the internet. Here are two pictures taken from the same viewpoint: Mount Scopus, near Jerusalem." He showed a picture of Jerusalem with many trees and looking quite fertile. Then he showed a very dry scene, all rocks and barren earth. "Look one way," he continued, "and you see the city. Look the other and you see the wilderness where Jesus was tempted."

Matthew then turned to the CD player. "You can buy discs with recordings of Bible stories. This is the story of the Good Samaritan with the innkeeper as the main character. You can listen to it after the lesson if you like - it only lasts ten minutes."

After they had spent about twenty minutes trying out the different kinds of equipment, Matthew asked the group to sit down.

"All these pieces of equipment," he said, "are called

'teaching aids'. He held up a clear piece of plastic with some writing on it. This sheet is called a 'transparency'."

He put the transparency on the glass plate of the O.H.P. and turned on the light. The screen in front lit up and the class read the printed chart.

TEACHING AIDS

Some are expensive, and need electricity
Laptop or smartphone with projector
CD player
Television with DVDs and Camcorder (Video Camera)
Overhead Projector (O.H.P.) with transparencies

Cheap and easy to use
Blackboard
Flipchart
Flannelgraph
Pictures, Maps, Diagrams

"There are other teaching aids," continued Matthew, "but the ones on the screen are the most common. The problem is, most of the modern aids are expensive or need special pens and paper. Business firms and colleges can use them but small groups of people just don't have the money. Also, as you see, the first four need an electricity supply. If you haven't got electricity, you can't afford them.

"The islands where Ayung teaches have no electricity," continued Matthew, " so I asked him to lead a discussion on the kind of teaching aids he might be able to use with his classes. Ayung, would you like to take over?"

Ayung moved his chair so that he faced the semi-circle of students. Matthew had been in touch with Ayung during the week. They had discussed together the main points he would bring up. Ayung began by repeating some of the information he had given the group at their first meeting.

"About a year ago, I was teaching in the secondary school in the biggest town of the island on which I live. As you know, I am a Catholic and usually go to Mass every week. One Sunday, after the service, our Parish priest asked me if I would consider doing a very important full-time job for the church. I said I was quite happy doing my present job and had no plans to leave it, but if the job was really important, I would consider it. The priest arranged for me to see the Bishop. The Bishop told me he needed someone to go to the different villages in the islands and train leaders of local congregations. He wanted leaders who would look after the congregations and build them up. I told the Bishop I was not qualified for that kind of job. A priest should do it. But the Bishop said he had no priests to spare.

"I asked him what resources he could give me. He said he could let me have a boat. He would give me a training manual and a very small budget to buy paper and other equipment. He offered to pay me the same salary I was getting as a teacher so my family would not be any worse off. And he said this job was a pilot scheme. If it was successful, then I would be put in charge of a full Diocesan training scheme so more villages could be helped.

"I thought about this very carefully and discussed it with my wife and also with my children. They are ten and thirteen years old so I thought they should be involved. We prayed together. Eventually I decided quite simply that God was calling me to this job. My family agreed with me so I told the Bishop I would do it. I am sure it was right, because the school was able to find another Mathematics teacher to replace me when I left three months ago. And you know how hard it is to get teachers of Mathematics! I have about twenty villages to visit on three islands and so far I have visited five of them. It's a hard task and I have to be away from home for days at a time, but I think I am doing the right thing."

The others listened with deep interest as Ayung spoke. They realised again that he and his family must have made a great sacrifice when he started this work. They also saw what a lonely job it was sailing to these isolated villages where he had to win the confidence of the people he was trying to help.

"This gives you the background of what I am trying to do," continued Ayung. "Matthew asked me to discuss with you what kind of teaching aids I could use with these groups of people. Only two of the villages have electricity and I have very little money to spend. So there is no way I could use most of these pieces of equipment even if there was money to buy them."

"Could I interrupt for a moment?" said Matthew. "It would help if we could think of just one typical village. Perhaps you could describe a village for us and give us an idea of the kind of group we're thinking about."

Ayung thought for a moment. "I'll tell you about a village called Karamu," he said. "There are just over one hundred people living in and around the village. Twenty-five of them are children. There is a small primary school looked after by a young teacher. He is not very happy as he comes from a town. The Government paid for his training and for three years he has to go where the Government sends him. The village is by the sea. The houses are mostly built on stilts and some are over the sea. They do not have any electricity but there is a stream running down to the beach which gives them fresh water. Most of the men are fishermen. There are some small fields where they can grow vegetables and rice. There are no shops but there is a path to a larger village with three shops. It takes two hours to walk there. Five years ago, the Government said they would build a road, but the people are still waiting!

"About thirty of the adults are Christians and they meet in the school. A priest comes about once every two months to say Mass and baptise any new converts. The Christians have chosen ten people to form a group to lead the church. I have to train them to lead worship, to pray for the sick, to prepare people for baptism and to lead Bible study groups. They also want training in evangelism so they can persuade other members of the village to become Christians.

"I think that gives you a picture of a typical village. Now I am going to pass Matthew's question to you. What kind of teaching aids could I use?"

"Do you have a blackboard?" asked Margaret.

"The school in this village has one. The Bishop has offered me a supply of chalk!"

"Good for the Bishop!" said Margaret. "But seriously, although all these wonderful pieces of equipment you see in this room are useful, I still think the blackboard is the best help to teaching that there is. It is cheap. You can use it for headings, lists and diagrams and for longer bits of writing. You can even draw good pictures if you have some coloured chalk. Perhaps you could carry one in your boat to take to villages which don't have schools."

"You mean you can do as much with a blackboard as you can with all these other things?" asked Dominic.

"Not quite as much," said Margaret. "But you can be an excellent teacher without all these modern gadgets."

"Another useful teaching aid," said Matthew, "is a flannelgraph. It's cheap and anyone can make one."

"How do you make a flannelgraph?" asked Nancy.

"All you need," said Matthew, "is a piece of rough cloth, like a blanket, fastened to a board. Then some other coarse material; preferably a few pieces in different colours. Cut out figures from this material to stick to your board."

"Have the people got Bibles?" asked Nancy, "And, are they able to read them?"

"Six out of the ten can read," replied Ayung. "I have been given a supply of New Testaments in their own language by a foreign charity. I'll sell them to the people at a low price. They will take more care of them if they buy them."

"Do the Bibles have pictures?" asked Jenny.

"No," said Ayung. "But my own does and I can take that with me."

"Can you get hold of any other pictures?" asked Solomon.

"I have a few, but they are very Western. Jesus is pictured as a white man with blue eyes and long flowing hair. I'm sure he didn't look like that!"

"You could use that to discuss what Jesus really did look like," replied Solomon. "But I could give you a few more modern pictures that might help. How about paper? Do you have paper and pens?"

"I have some," replied Ayung. "But it is difficult to keep paper dry in the boat and, as I said, some of the group can't write."

"You know," said Theresa, "the best teaching aid you have is the group you are working with. You can do all sorts of things with people."

"What do you mean?" asked Ayung.

"Well, I often don't have a blackboard or suitable pictures," Theresa explained. "The people are too poor and I don't even have a budget like you do. So I use the people. For example, suppose we have to go to a Government office to try and get them to build public toilets; I get one woman to be the person in the office. Then I get another to be the official we have to see. The woman in the office is very rude and won't let us in. We discuss how we might get past her to the more important official."

"You could do that when you are teaching stories from the Bible," said Nancy. "If you were teaching the story about healing the leper, ask someone to pretend to be the leper. How would he feel? What sort of life would he lead? What would the others think of him?"

"Or if you are teaching them about visiting the sick," added Solomon, "ask one of the group to lie down on a mat and pretend to be sick. Then get the group to discuss who would go to see him. What would they say? How would they pray? It's like doing a role play that we talked about some time ago."

"There's another way of using the people in the group," added Matthew. "If you haven't a blackboard, or if the people can't read, ask each person to remember one heading. Then at the end of the lesson, each person tells the others what the heading is. For example, when we were learning about planning a lesson, I could have told you, Nancy, to remember the word 'Introduction'. You, Dominic, 'Aim'. You, Ayung, 'Main part of lesson'. Finally, I would ask you, Solomon, to remember 'Conclusion'. At the end of the lesson, I would ask each one of you to say what your heading was. And I would ask you to say just a sentence or two to remind people why each heading is important. That would take the place of a summary on the blackboard. Use the students to sum up your lesson."

"Another, quite different, way of using your students," said Margaret, "is to use their talents. For example, if one is good at carving, you could get him to carve the figure of Jesus on the cross. Then he and the group could discuss what it meant to them. That would be an excellent visual aid, even if the carving wasn't very good."

"That's three different ways of using the members of the group!" said Ayung. "Can you think of any other teaching aids I can use?"

"Could you use the things you have around you?" asked Theresa. "Things like the trees and the beach and the fields. The disciples of Jesus were fishermen, so your villagers must have a lot in common with them."

"That's an important point," said Matthew. "Jesus was one of the best teachers the world has ever known. He didn't have a blackboard or any other kind of gadget. He didn't even have a Bible. He learnt the passages from the Old Testament as a boy. The synagogues would have scrolls of the Law and of the Prophets so Jesus would hear readings from these every Sabbath. But Jesus used trees, the fields, harvesting, fishing and village life to teach important lessons. It is one of the very powerful traditional ways of teaching, especially for country people. Country people are very used to listening to stories and remembering them."

Margaret said, "You know, one of the best ways of teaching

about the resurrection would be to actually relive the stories. You could take your class onto the beach. One of the villagers could build a fire and cook some fish. That would be a wonderful teaching aid! And perhaps you could have a quiet time of prayer asking them to imagine Jesus actually being with them."

"Thank you, for all those suggestions," said Ayung. "I'll try to use them with my groups. Just a moment while I sum up what we have said. I'll use the blackboard as Margaret suggested."

"Try using different coloured chalks," said Margaret. "See if it makes it more interesting."

They laughed as Ayung wrote on the blackboard:

Teaching Aids for a village

Blackboard
Bibles - especially one with pictures
Pens and paper
Flannelgraph
Things that are around: beach, trees, stones, etc.
The students themselves.
They can:
Pretend to be characters in a story
Remember headings
Use their talents

Matthew brought the lesson to a close.

"Thank you very much, Ayung, for leading the discussion," he said. "I hope that has given you some ideas to use in your lessons. Remember! You do not need fancy teaching aids to be good teachers. Often, when the students are poor, it's better to keep to simple things. It could be very discouraging for poor students if you often used expensive teaching aids. Has anyone any other comments?"

He paused for a moment, but no one could think of anything more to say.

"Right," said Matthew. "I think it is Margaret's turn to lead our prayers."

Lessons to learn from this chapter

A TEACHING AID is a piece of equipment that helps you when you are teaching.

DIFFERENT TEACHING AIDS

<u>Expensive and need electricity</u>

1. Computer or smartphone with projector
2. CD player with CDs
3. Overhead projector with transparencies
4. Television with Video Camera and DVDs (Digital Video Disc)

<u>Cheap and simple</u>

5. Blackboard (coloured chalks can be useful)
6. Flipchart
7. Flannelgraph
8. Pictures, maps, diagrams
9. Bibles, especially with pictures (be careful if not all can read)
10. The students themselves:
    - Acting as characters in a training session or bible story
    - Remembering lesson headings
    - Using their talents (Drawing, Carving etc.)
11. Everyday things like stones, rocks, water, streams to illustrate sayings like "the Lord is my rock and my fortress", "streams of living water..."

You may be able to borrow equipment. Make sure you can use any equipment properly before teaching your lesson!

Your lessons will be more interesting if you can use different teaching aids.

Chapter 10

Dominic has a problem with his group

Dominic took the earlier bus to Matthew's house. He felt he had to have a talk with Matthew before the others arrived. He was feeling quite depressed. As soon as Matthew opened the door Dominic asked, "Can I talk to you?"

"Of course," said Matthew. "It looks as if you have had a bad day. What is the trouble?"

"It wasn't today," said Dominic. "It was my class last night. I had quite a good lesson planned. At least, I thought it was good. But almost before I started, one person went into a great speech about how Jesus was going to come back to earth soon. He said that it was all written in the book of Revelation. He just wouldn't stop talking. I tried to stop him but some of the others joined in and started arguing with him. We went round and round in circles. Every time I went back to my lesson, he found some way of interrupting. It was a complete waste of the evening. I'm worried that some members got so bored they won't come again. I don't think I'm very good at teaching adults after all."

"How many good lessons have you had?" asked Matthew.

"We've had five sessions so far and four have gone well. But this person has only come to the last two. He thought I wasn't teaching them the true Gospel because I had not said anything about the Second Coming. He went on and on about the coming of Jesus and how we would all be judged. He said the signs were right for it to happen very soon and he asked us if we were all prepared to meet Jesus. I couldn't stop him talking."

"Alright," said Matthew, "you have had one bad lesson out of five. The members of your group won't give up because of one bad lesson. But, of course, you can't let it happen again. Why not put your problem to the members of our group and see if they can give you some ideas?"

"But they'll think I can't control my class or teach properly!" exclaimed Dominic.

"They won't," replied Matthew. "Just do it and see what their reaction is. I think you'll find you get a lot of sympathy."

A few minutes later the room filled up. Matthew had thought about Dominic's problem and decided to change his lesson. He decided to bring forward the lesson he had planned for the following week. It was a lesson about leading small groups. Dominic's problem was a very good way of introducing the subject and Matthew was sure all the students would find it interesting.

"Dominic has just come up with a very important problem that many teachers have to face," he said. "I want you to see if you can help him solve it. Dominic, will you explain what happened at your teaching session last night?"

Dominic took a deep breath and told them his problem. He described how one member of the group had disrupted his class and spoilt his carefully prepared lesson. He said he was afraid that some of the group would not come back. He was very worried about facing the group again if this particular person was going to be present.

"You know," said Theresa, "I had exactly the same problem a few months ago with one of the women in my group. She just wouldn't stop talking. She was going on and on about how it was useless to try and do anything. 'We are just wasting our time,' she said. 'Things are hopeless and the authorities don't care.' I just couldn't continue with the lesson at all."

"What happened?" asked Nancy.

"Eventually this woman started to cry. One of the mothers went up and put her arms round her. It turned out that her two little children had died of dysentery and, although it had happened a year ago, she was still grieving deeply. Some of the mothers who had also lost children were able to help her. She is much better now. She still comes to my classes."

"That must have been awful," said Nancy. "Do many children die where you live?"

"Almost every day," replied Theresa. "Two days ago, an eleven-year-old boy was stabbed to death. They think he woke up when burglars were robbing the house and the robbers killed him because he saw them. It is very hard. I worry a lot about my own little boy. He could so easily get sick or have an accident when he is playing. Sometimes I am tempted to give up. But then I think of the good things we have done and so I go on with the work. Dominic, I don't think you should be discouraged by one bad lesson."

"I can understand about the mother who had lost her children," replied Dominic. "But I don't understand the man in my class. He just seems obsessed with the teaching that Jesus is going to come again."

"But Jesus is going to come again," said Nancy.

"We all believe that," said Matthew, "but that isn't the problem that Dominic has. The problem is how to deal with a person who dominates your group. How do you get a person to stop talking about whatever he, or she, is determined to talk about? Have you any suggestions that might help Dominic?"

"I wonder," said Ayung, "what is making him talk so much about the Second Coming?"

"Some just like the sound of their own voice," said Solomon. "I have a similar problem. I followed Matthew's advice and started letting the class discuss things more. The trouble is that there's one man who always has a lot to say, usually about the same thing. It is very hard to shut him up. I'd like to ask him to leave the group but I can't do that without a lot of trouble. It was much easier when I just dictated notes and none of them spoke except to ask a few questions!"

Matthew laughed. "There are times when I would like to go back to the old days and simply lecture. It is easier for the teacher. But if we want students to think for themselves, we must have time for discussion. And we will get people who want to talk and talk. Have any of you had other kinds of problems with people in your group?"

"My problem is quite the opposite," said Margaret. "I'm worried about the mice."

The others looked at her with astonishment. Mice in the classroom!

"I don't mean real mice," said Margaret. "I mean the students who are like mice. They never make a sound! They are too shy to join in. The only way to get them to talk is to ask them direct questions. Then they blush and shuffle around. I think they are afraid they'll give stupid answers."

"I've got a different problem," said Ayung. "At Karamu, the village medicine man is in my group. Some people might call him a witch doctor. The other members of the group always look at him to see if he is going to speak before they will say anything. And if he does speak, no one dares to disagree with him. It isn't that he always talks. It's just that when he does say something, he thinks he's right and so does everyone else. Even when they think he's wrong, they are too frightened to say anything that might contradict him!"

"You see, Dominic," said Matthew, "you are not the only one with problems among their groups of students. We all have students who can be difficult at times. So we all have to learn how to deal with them. The best way is to help the student to become a willing and useful member of the group.

"So what can Dominic do with this person who will not stop talking about the Second Coming? Dominic needs an answer because he has to face his class again next week."

"Could you go to see him in his own home?" asked Nancy. "Then you would find out more about him and why he feels so strongly about the Second Coming of Jesus. There are some churches that teach about that and almost nothing else. Maybe he has come from one of those churches. Find out what is on his mind. Then, perhaps, you can tell him that the Second Coming, although very important, is not the only teaching of the Christian faith."

"I'll try that," said Dominic. "But what if he still goes on?"

Margaret said, "It could be that he is suffering from an illness called 'depression'. It's an illness of the mind. Often, when people suffer from depression, things go round and round their minds and they can't think of anything else."

"How can you cure it?" asked Nancy.

"You need to go to hospital and get special drugs," replied Margaret. "But I do know of people suffering from depression who have been cured by prayer."

"But there is another way of dealing with a person who talks all the time," she continued, "and that is to get the group to help. Ask one or two members of the group to interrupt him and say, politely, 'We have heard you say all this before, so can we move on to something else?' Or you could say to the group, 'Is anyone else interested in talking about this subject now?' If no one is, say, 'Let's move on.'"

"What if two or three say they want to talk about it?" asked Dominic.

"Then," replied Margaret, "take a vote on it. If most want to move on, do that. If most want to talk about the subject, tell the group you are happy to spend half an hour on the topic."

"So, Dominic," said Matthew, "we've made some suggestions. Do you think any of them are helpful?"

"I'll try going to see him and find out what his problems are," replied Dominic. "I think that's the best suggestion. I'll also tell him and the other members of the group that we will be talking about the Second Coming of Jesus later in the course. That should help those who want to talk about it in more detail. They won't feel I'm ignoring their questions."

"But a teacher can't go to see all the members of the class," said Nancy, "especially if it is a large class."

"No," said Matthew. "But not all members of your classes have problems of that kind. Also, you must remember that part of teaching is pastoral work. The teacher is also a carer so it would be right, if Dominic has the time, to go and see this particular person."

"What can I do about my medicine man?" asked Ayung. "The people are too afraid to contradict him."

"Are you frightened of him?" asked Theresa.

"I've thought about that quite a lot. I know a Christian shouldn't be afraid of spells, but he is a very powerful man. If he threatened to put a spell on one of my children, I would be afraid. But, of course, he hasn't done anything like that."

"I once had a spell put on me," said Nancy. "I was supposed to die after the magic words had been said. It was very frightening. I've never prayed so hard in my life!"

"Did you go to another person to get the spell lifted?" asked Ayung.

"No! I trusted that the power of Jesus was greater," Nancy replied. "But I don't know what I would have done if he had threatened my children."

"I think it is better, with such a powerful person, to avoid challenging him directly," said Matthew. "I know that may seem like being a coward, but confrontation might well destroy the whole group. So you would lose anyway. But, having said that, we must remember that there is the story in the Acts of the Apostles about St. Paul confronting Elymas the Sorcerer.

Let's try to think what Ayung can do."

"How convinced a Christian is he?" asked Margaret.

"Difficult to say," answered Ayung. "I am still not sure whether he is in the church because he genuinely believes in Jesus. He may be coming because he wants to hold on to his power even in the church."

"Again, I think it would be good to have a private talk with him," said Margaret. "I think your main task is to find out more about his faith. If he really does believe, then you can approach the problem by discussing what God is calling him to do as a Christian in the village. If not, then I think you will have to try another approach."

"What could that be?" asked Ayung.

"I can think of two possibilities," answered Margaret. "The first is to give him a chance of leading the group on a subject that he knows about. For example, ask him to give a talk on the subject 'What is the role of the medicine man in a Christian Ministry Team?' That might make him say what he really thinks. The other way is to have a Bible study. Let the Bible speak to him.

"The Holy Spirit really is powerful and can do amazing things. You could use St. Paul's letter to the Romans, Chapter Twelve, where Paul tells Christians how they should treat each other. Ask the group to work out what it means in practice. How should they treat each other and members of the church? What are the particular gifts of each person in the group? And bring in the witch doctor. Ask him what it means in practice to love a fellow Christian. What would he do if someone asks him to put a spell on another person? There is great power in the words of the Bible itself. If you're not sure about using the letter to the Romans, try studying the story of Jesus washing the feet of the disciples."

"I think you need help with this," said Matthew. "Before you do anything, discuss the matter with your priest or your Bishop. We all need support at times. If I have a really serious problem in the college, I talk to the Principal before I do anything. Perhaps the Bishop can help you to work out a strategy so you will have some backing. However, I am quite certain that God has called you to do this work. He will provide a way of solving this problem. Your witch doctor could become your strongest worker. It's happened before. But we should all pray regularly for you and the villagers of Karamu."

"Can we do that tonight?" asked Dominic. "And also pray for my problem and for Theresa that she may be encouraged in the work she is doing?"

"Of course," said Matthew. "But first let me sum up what we have said."

Matthew wrote on his blackboard:

Possible ways of dealing with difficult people in a class
1. **Talk to them, if possible in their homes.**
2. **Find out what their real problem is.**
3. **Get the group to gently deal with them.**
4. **Firmly, but politely say, "We must move on."**
5. **Pray for such people.**
6. **Lead a Bible study, especially a passage about loving one another.**
7. **The person may be depressed and may need expert help.**
8. **Discuss the problem with your superior or a person you can trust.**

"Thank you, Dominic, for bringing up your problem," said Matthew. "It has helped us all. We will be thinking about it next week when I am going to discuss how a group develops and grows."

"Excuse me," interrupted Margaret, "but what about my mice?"

"I haven't forgotten them," said Matthew. "In the next lesson we will think of ways to encourage the quiet ones to speak. Now let's pray for each other and especially for difficult people in our classes."

Lessons to learn from this chapter

1. If you have a problem, share it with someone you can trust. You will find other people have similar problems.

2. Groups of people who are studying together often contain difficult people. In fact we can all be difficult at times! But when a person tries to dominate the group so that the others cannot learn, the teacher has to find a way of stopping him.

3. Ways of helping such a person:
    (a) Talk to him or her.
    (b) Find out if he or she has any problems.
    (c) Get the group to help you.
    (d) If the group wants to discuss a subject someone has raised, set a time limit.
    (e) Use Bible study.
    (f) Get back-up.

4. Pray for your students, especially those with difficulties.

Chapter 11

More about leading small groups

Group members as the leader sees them:

1. The Quarrelsome Type: Don't get involved; stop him/her monopolising the team.
2. The Positive Type: Great help in discussion, use often.
3. The Know-All Type: Let group deal with him/her.
4. The Talkative Type: Interrupt tactfully, limit speaking time.
5. The Shy Type: Ask easy questions; give encouragement to increase confidence.
6. The Unco-operative/hostile type: Recognise knowledge and experience and use them.
7. The Thick-Skinned/Uninterested Type: Discover interests and strengths and use them.
8. The Highbrow/Academic Type: Don't criticise openly – use, "yes, but have you thought about…" technique.
9. The Persistent Questioner: Tries to trap teacher - pass the suggestions back to the group.

When they arrived at Matthew's house for the next lesson, Dominic was secretly relieved to see that the chairs were arranged as normal. There didn't seem to be any surprises. Then he noticed that on each chair was a sheet of paper with a picture on it with the heading, 'Group members as the leader sees them'.

Nancy and Margaret were looking at the picture and laughing. Dominic went to one of the chairs and picked up a paper. The others came in and, when they saw the papers, picked them up to have a look.

"There's my witch doctor," said Ayung. "Number six. He can be friendly but when someone disagrees with him, he looks just like that. All prickly."

"I've got a number three in my group," said Nancy. "He's got answers to everything. The only trouble is that his answers simply don't work."

"There's my mice," said Margaret. "I've got two number fives in my class."

Just then, Matthew came in. They all sat down, still looking at the pictures and reading the comments.

"Well," he said, "What do you think? Are the suggestions any help?"

"No," said Margaret. "It says here about the shy ones, 'ask easy questions'. I've tried that! They know the answers but they are still too shy to speak out."

"I don't think you should do any more," commented Matthew. "If you try to make them talk, you will probably embarrass them too much and they will stop coming to classes. Be patient with them and leave it to them to decide when they would like to talk."

"I think you are right," said Margaret. "I must try to understand what they are feeling and not force them into doing something they are afraid to do. Perhaps I could find other ways of encouraging them."

"I don't think the suggestion for number four would have helped at the start," said Dominic. "But I did what you suggested at the last lesson. I went to see him. He feels very guilty about leaving his other church. He admitted he was trying to feel good about it by trying to find out if other people thought the same as he did. When I asked him what he really thought, he realised he wasn't as sure as pretended to be. I think I could use the suggestion 'interrupt tactfully' if he started talking again about the Second Coming."

"I'm glad that worked out alright," said Matthew. "But now, look again at the different types of people which make up a group. The characters in the picture are exaggerated, but we can all recognise that people are to some extent like those in the diagram. However, I'm going to ask you an embarrassing question. Do you recognise yourself in any of those characters?"

There was a bit of a silence as the group studied the pictures again. Theresa was the one to break the silence. "I'm not sure if I'm really there, but I know I talk too much. I could be a bit like number four but I hope I don't sound like a frog!"

"I was very shy at the beginning," said Dominic. "But Matthew has been very good at encouraging me. I'm not afraid of saying what I think anymore."

"I thought you were very academic like number eight," said Nancy to Solomon. "But now I've got to know you better, I know you're not really. Not in a way that puts anyone off."

"I suppose I would always like to be number two, the positive type," said Margaret. "But there are times when I am more like number six, unco-operative. Especially when I disagree completely with a proposal."

"Thank you for those comments," said Matthew. "Think a bit more about it when you get home. Now I am going to change the subject. I want you to think about how you and the group have changed. If you have a good group like this one, you'll find that people change as they learn together. And that applies to the difficult people in your groups as well. Every person has good points as well as bad. Even the prickly ones can change and become very helpful members of a group. Also remember that you, as leader, will change as well. So, in this lesson, we are going to think about how groups work. The English word is a rather difficult one. The word is 'dynamics'. It comes from an old Greek word meaning 'power' and is used frequently in the Bible. When we use the word in connection with groups of people, we mean the power or energy that is at work in the group."

Matthew wrote on the board:

GROUP DYNAMICS

"These two words are often used in the context of teaching adults, but you don't need to go too deeply into their meaning. Just remember it is about how people in a group interact with each other and about how they influence each other.

"Now I want you to learn about this by looking at our own group. We are going to think about how this group has progressed. In other words, we are going to look at the 'Group Dynamics' of this class.

"Can any of you remember how we first started?"

"I remember we all introduced ourselves and explained a bit about what we did," said Nancy.

"That seems a long time ago," said Theresa. "Just think, we were all strangers then."

"But before that," said Matthew, "before you even started coming here."

"My church asked me if I would like to be a member of a class that was learning how to teach adults," said Dominic. "They said it would help me to lead my group of beginners in the Christian faith. I thought about it and agreed to come."

"As you know, it was my Bishop who asked me to come," said Ayung. "I had to think very carefully as it meant leaving my family for some time. But my wife thought I should go. I was very interested because I thought the course would help with the work I was starting. It certainly has done that."

Solomon agreed with Ayung. "My Bishop asked me to come," he said.

"My District Supervisor asked me," said Nancy. "He was impressed with my work as an evangelist and asked me if I would train others." She turned to Margaret, asking, "How did you come to be on the course?"

"When Matthew told me he was hoping to start this

course," replied Margaret, "I volunteered. It was such a good idea that I didn't want to be left out."

"So," said Matthew, "the first stage for any group is actually forming the group. This must be done carefully. It can be done in different ways, for example by advertising or by invitation. But the people in the group must want to learn whatever the course is about. So the first word I can write down is:

FORMING

"Next, as Nancy said, we met each other and introduced ourselves."

"You also outlined the course," said Ayung. "That helped me a lot. I didn't really know what I was coming to and I felt much better when you explained what we were going to do."

"The mini-lessons we gave were very interesting. I think it really brought the group together, especially when we had to think of something good to say about each other," said Margaret.

"OK," said Matthew. "I'm going to sum up 'getting to know each other' and 'getting to know the content of the course' by a word which rhymes with 'forming' and that is:

INFORMING

"After that, some of you weren't very happy with the way things were going. You were one of them, Dominic."

Dominic blushed.

"I was being stupid," he said. "I thought you weren't teaching us anything."

"You weren't being stupid," said Matthew. "You were, in fact, being helpful. You said something that many others were thinking and so you brought out into the open a very real problem. Now that is extremely important. Every group will have tensions in it. This is bound to happen when people work together. As we saw in the last lesson, your own groups have had their difficulties. If the tensions are hidden under the surface, they can be very destructive and not much progress can be made. If the problems are faced and worked through, things really change."

"You know," said Solomon, "I agreed with Dominic so much that at that time I nearly left the group."

The others looked at Solomon in astonishment.

"You were going to leave?" asked Margaret.

"Yes," Solomon replied. "I thought I was wasting my time and went to see the Bishop. The Bishop persuaded me to stay. Actually he asked me to stay and priests don't disobey their Bishops, at least, not without very good reason! I'm really glad I stayed."

"And I am very glad you made that decision," said Matthew. "But what you and Dominic have said does illustrate an important principle. Most groups have to go through a stormy period. It may be early on like this one, or it may come later in the life of the group. If the stormy time is used constructively, it can be of great help. Otherwise it really can destroy the group.

"Of course, if the teacher simply stands in front of the class and lectures, the class won't have the chance to go through that experience. But students still feel things inside themselves and, while they can learn facts, they don't really learn much about themselves. So if you have a group, especially a small one, expect trouble at some time. If this happens, don't get disheartened. Remember it can be a very useful help to progress. So we had a disagreement, a bit of a 'storm'. And I am going to call this stage STORMING."

They all laughed as Matthew wrote the word in bold letters on the board, thinking back to how uneasy they were at that time and how relaxed they were now.

"What came next?" asked Matthew.

"I suppose we just settled down and got on with the job," said Ayung.

"Yes," said Nancy. "I think we've worked together well."

"I could write that down as you have said it," replied Matthew. "But to keep the rhyme going I'm going to use two words. You will find the first word in a good dictionary but it is not often used."

Matthew wrote on the board the words:

NORMING (settling down)
PERFORMING (working together)

"Not all groups go through these stages but this is often the pattern. Using the rhyming words makes it easier to remember. If you don't like the words, don't bother with them. Just remember that there are different stages to the life of every group. There is one more stage but I can't think of a word that rhymes with the others so I'll just have to write down:

ENDING

"Ending the life of a group can be difficult. People get to know each other well. When a course finishes they have to say goodbye to friends, as we will have to do. There is a feeling of loneliness, of being on your own. It doesn't happen if everyone lives in the same village but it can happen if people come from different places as you do. We will discuss how to end a course of lessons later.

"The other point is that to make the 'Performing' happen there must be two things. There must be a very good overall aim or target. Then there must be a good plan of the work to be covered. People need to be satisfied that they are making progress. This makes them happy with the course and they work well.

"The plan for the course is called a 'scheme of work' or 'a schedule of work.' We will be thinking about that in another session."

Matthew turned his board around and wrote on the other side:

NECESSARY FOR PERFORMING (FOR THE GROUP TO MAKE PROGRESS)

A CLEAR AIM AND A GOOD SCHEME OF WORK (PLAN OF LESSONS)

"Have you any questions before we start our prayers?"

Theresa asked, "What would you say your aim is for this group?"

"To help you become good teachers of adults," replied Matthew. "Or I could say, good 'Adult Educators'."

Solomon spoke. "I've been thinking about the different teaching methods you described. This lesson has been most interesting because you have used the life of this group to help us understand how groups work. I suppose you could call this a special kind of 'case study'."

"That's right," said Matthew. "I try to use different teaching methods in each of these classes. I thought I could use the life of this group as a good example of what is likely to happen whenever you teach small groups. So we have learnt a little about 'Group Dynamics' by looking at the 'dynamics' of our own group. But remember this group is an exceptionally good one and not all groups will follow the same pattern. Have you any other questions?"

No one had anything else to say so they turned to their prayers.

Lessons to learn from this chapter

1.   Every group is different and has a life of its own.

2. There will probably be difficult people in the group. Try to understand them and work out ways of helping them to become people who contribute rather than disrupt. Especially be very patient with those who are shy. Don't make them do anything they feel unable to do and find ways of giving them encouragement.

3. Most groups do go through stages:

    Forming   Coming together
    Informing   Getting to know each other
    Storming   Having difficulties and disagreements
    Norming   Working through these difficulties
    Performing Working together
    Ending   It is important to work out a good way to end the course

4. Not all groups will go through all these stages. For example, a group might work peacefully together for the whole of the course.

5. Members of the group need to have confidence in the progress of the course. Clear aims and a good plan of lessons (scheme of work) are important.

Chapter 12

Dominic and Theresa meet to plan their lesson

Dominic felt his heart beating faster as he climbed the stairs leading to Theresa's flat. He really was becoming very attracted to her and wondered if she felt the same about him. He remembered that it was not safe for anyone to open the door to strangers. So, as he knocked on the door, he called out, "It's Dominic."

Theresa opened the door to him and seemed really pleased to see him. "I've got some coffee," she said. "Would you like a drink?"

"Yes, thank you," he replied, looking at Benedict who was fast asleep on a small mattress.

"It's all right," Theresa said. "Once he falls asleep, he's difficult to wake. We can talk without disturbing him."

Dominic was about to say something more, but as Theresa handed him the coffee, she went straight to the point.

"Let's get down to work," she said. "Matthew asked us to teach a lesson as if we were teaching it to one of our own small groups. Have you had any ideas?"

"Not really," Dominic replied. "But let's first think of the people in our classes. I am teaching a group of ten men. The youngest is sixteen and the oldest is sixty. They've all just been converted to Christianity and I have to teach them what it means to be a Christian. I have a book to follow so I don't need to make up lessons of my own. But what I have learnt from Matthew has helped me to make my lessons more interesting."

"Well, apart from my literacy classes," replied Theresa, "all my groups are women. Although I have some notes to guide me, I really have to plan each session myself. I am supposed to teach primary health care but there are many different issues that come up. The sewer was one. Then there's housing, schools for children, malnutrition and the job situation. The women are trying to get the Government to do all kinds of things, but we haven't had much success so far. We've got a half promise about a school in the area but on the whole it's slow progress. At times we get very disheartened.

"Do you really think we can find something suitable for both your men and my women? Mind you, some of my single women might like to meet your younger men. And the older ones too, if they've got some money!"

Dominic laughed as he thought of one of his sixty year olds teaming up with a young mother with four kids. Then he had an idea. "I wonder if you could do a Bible study."

"No!" said Theresa firmly. Only half of them are Christian and the other half would leave if I tried to get them to be Christians."

"I am not thinking about trying to get them to be Christians," replied Dominic. "I was thinking about one of the passages from the Bible. It's a passage that might encourage your group when they get disheartened. Even if they are not Christians, they might be interested in what Jesus says."

"I am not sure some of them would," said Theresa. "But show me the passage and I'll think about it. I've got a Bible here."

Together they looked at some verses from St. Luke's Gospel, Chapter Four. These verses told how Jesus gave a reading from the book of the Prophet Isaiah to the Jews in the synagogue at Capernaum. Although Theresa had heard the reading before, she hadn't thought of applying it to her little group of women. Now, as she read the words Jesus himself had spoken, her heart quickened:

> "The Spirit of the Lord is on me,
> because he has anointed me
> to preach good news to the poor.
> He has sent me to proclaim freedom for the prisoners
> and recovery of sight for the blind,
> to release the oppressed,
> to proclaim the year of the Lord's favour."

Dominic and Theresa went on to read how the congregation were very impressed at first. But when Jesus said something that displeased them, they turned against him and tried to throw him over a cliff. Theresa was all too familiar with this kind of rejection. It almost seemed as though the reading was saying something to her.

"I like that," she said. "I think I might make something of it. It's different from anything I have done before with my class but maybe it will work. Let's do it as a Bible Study with Matthew's group and if it goes down well, I can try it with my women. My main problem is actually introducing it to my group of women. Some of them will be very suspicious if I start reading the Bible to them."

"I don't have that problem with my men," said Dominic. "They've been told to read the Bible regularly now they have become Christians. But it will help me to teach the passage to them if we work out a lesson together."

He thought for a moment and then said, "I think there is a way you could introduce it to your group if they really trust and like you. Why not start by saying that there have been times when you have been really down-hearted and discouraged. But this passage has really helped you and given you new hope. Because of that, you would like to pass it on to them. If they do not seem interested you can just tell them you'll forget the idea. But I think they will want to hear more. Use your good relationship with them to introduce something new."

"That kind of introduction might work," said Theresa. "We have become very close after that mother told us about her children dying. Let's do a plan and see if it will work out."

Together they worked on a lesson plan and decided who should teach the different parts of it. After an hour, they felt reasonably satisfied. It was getting late but Dominic didn't want to leave. In fact he longed to take Theresa in his arms. Like many of his friends, Dominic had been with girls before he became a Christian. Since then, it hadn't seemed right. And the elders were very strict about contact between the sexes. But now the teaching of the elders didn't seem all that important.

"Theresa!" he stammered. She rushed to him and they clung together. Just then Benedict stirred and sat up. Theresa and Dominic sprang apart as Benedict opened his eyes. He smiled as his sight focused on Dominic.

"Hello!" he said

"Hello!" said Dominic, "You go back to sleep. I'm just going."

Theresa went to the door with him. "He hasn't woken up like that for months," she said. "Once he's asleep nothing wakes him."

"Perhaps God was trying to tell us something," said Dominic. "Let's take it a bit more slowly, but we must meet more often." He kissed her again, this time on her cheek. "See you at Matthew's."

Lessons to learn from this chapter

1. Make sure that your subject matter is important to those you are teaching. If there are difficulties with this, think of a good way of introducing the subject.

2. Friendships will be formed between members of your class - sometimes these will be very deep friendships!

3. If you are teaching a lesson with another person, make a detailed and careful plan so that each person knows what part of the lesson they have to teach.

NOTE: See Appendix D for Theresa's and Dominic's lesson plan.

Chapter 13

A demonstration lesson by Dominic and Theresa

Later that week, they met at Matthew's house for the next lesson. Matthew started the session. There were no surprises this time but they noticed that one of Matthew's cupboards had been moved against the wall in front of them. His table was in front of the cupboard with a space between the two. Matthew introduced the lesson very simply by saying that Theresa and Dominic would lead the class.

Dominic stood up.

"As you know," he said, "I teach a class of about ten men aged sixteen to sixty. Theresa leads a number of groups. One of these is made up of up to twenty women, some married, some with children. Their ages range from eighteen to forty. All of them are very poor and about half are Christians. Most of the women can read a little as a result of Theresa's literacy classes, but only about a third can read well.

"We did wonder if we could combine the groups. Theresa thought some of her women would be very happy to meet my men, especially the rich ones! After a lot of thought we decided to plan a lesson for Theresa's group, but the lesson would be a Bible study that I could teach to my group. The passage we have chosen is one of the most important in the New Testament. It sums up what Jesus taught about his work.

"So we would like you to imagine that you are one of the women in Theresa's group. Please pretend to be one of these very poor women. What would you think and feel as you study the passage? Theresa is going to lead the study and I am going to be one of the women!"

They all laughed at this and Theresa started speaking as though she was speaking to the women of her class.

"As you know, I'm a Christian. I believe in Jesus Christ. And I read the Bible, the Holy Book of Christians. The other day I came across a passage which really did seem to speak to me. I was feeling quite sad at the time and I do know some of you have been feeling disheartened. We don't seem to be getting very far with our work to improve living conditions. But this passage gave me new heart. It was so important to me that I want to tell you about it. Will you let me do that? I think the reading might encourage us all."

She paused and the rest of them nodded.

"The passage comes from a book of the Bible written by a person called Luke. The book is called the 'Gospel according to St. Luke'." Theresa held up her Bible with the page open at the beginning of St. Luke's Gospel. "But before we hear it read, I need to tell you a bit about the background. It took place in a synagogue. A synagogue is a place where the Jews meet to worship. It's a bit like a church but it is a Jewish church. At their worship, the Jews say or sing Psalms, the songs of the Bible. They have prayers. They have readings from the Bible and someone will give a talk. There is often time for questions and discussion. In the time of Jesus, they didn't have books like we do. They had scrolls. I will show you a scroll shortly. Written on the scrolls would be the books of the Law of God, teachings like 'Worship the Lord your God', 'Love your neighbour' and 'Do not steal'. In other scrolls were the writings of the prophets. Prophets are people who speak out on behalf of God. The prophets of the Bible tried to help people to keep God's law, but often the people would not listen to them. One of the most important prophets was called Isaiah."

Theresa held up the page of her Bible which showed the beginning of the book of the prophet Isaiah before continuing her talk.

"The scrolls were very expensive. They were written out by hand and were decorated with tassels. They were usually kept in a beautifully carved cupboard. In most synagogues, there was a reading desk in front of the scroll cupboard. This table is our reading desk. Now I am going to ask Margaret and then our sister, Dominic, to read the verses that we have chosen. Dominic will read the words that Jesus used and Margaret will read the introduction and other parts of the passage."

There was a laugh from the group as Dominic and Margaret stood up on one side. Dominic went to the table. Then the group listened carefully as Margaret read quietly but with such emphasis that every word seemed to have a special meaning.

"On the Sabbath day, Jesus went into the synagogue as was his custom. He stood up to read and the scroll of the Prophet Isaiah was handed to him."

She paused. Theresa went to the cupboard at the back of the room. She had made a scroll from sheets of white paper glued together and rolled up. She very reverently carried the scroll to the table and gave it to Dominic at the table. Dominic took his time as he carefully opened the scroll. The others could see rows of some kind of writing. Dominic pointed with his finger to the words he had copied onto the paper. He read the same words Jesus had read to the people in the synagogue at Nazareth.

> "The Spirit of the Lord is on me
> because he has anointed me
> to preach good news to the poor.
> He sent me to proclaim freedom for the prisoners
> and recovery of sight for the blind,
> to release the oppressed,
> to proclaim the year of the Lord's favour."

Margaret continued the reading, "Then he rolled up the scroll, gave it back to the attendant and sat down."

As she read this, Dominic rolled up the scroll and gave it to Theresa. Theresa very carefully put it back in the cupboard.

Margaret went on, "The eyes of everyone were fixed on Jesus and he began by saying to them…"

Dominic then sat down, looked around at them all and said, "Today, this scripture has been fulfilled in your hearing."

Margaret again took up the story with Dominic reading the words of Jesus. Dominic spoke about the many widows in Israel in Elijah's time, but that Elijah was sent to a foreigner in the land of Sidon. When Dominic came to the words of Jesus, "there were many lepers in Israel in the time of Elijah, yet not one was cleansed - only Naaman the Syrian," he paused.

Margaret continued, very dramatically, "All the people in the synagogue were furious when they heard this. They got up and took him to a hill in order to throw him down the cliff. But he walked right through the crowd and went on his way."

Theresa let the silence last for a few moments and slowly walked to the centre of the room.

"Let's imagine the scene, for a moment," she said. "You have seen the scroll opened and heard the reading. Now think again of Jesus opening the scroll and finding the place and reading those words. What do the words mean to you?" She paused for a short time and said, "Now think of Jesus saying that the prophet Elijah didn't heal Jews, but people who were not Jews, the widow and Naaman the leper. Suppose you were a Jew in that synagogue and believed that God was only concerned with you and other Jews. You, as a Jew, believe you are one of God's chosen people. Jesus is saying that God cares for other people as well. People you despise. Feel the anger among the congregation and then someone shouts, 'He's no prophet. This is blasphemy. He is insulting God.'" Theresa paused again. "Now imagine the crowd as some of them grab the arms of Jesus and rush him out on the hillside. Then see Jesus shaking himself free and walking through the crowd, leaving them to argue amongst themselves."

Theresa let the silence last a little longer and then continued, "Now I'm asking you to do just two things," she said. "The first is to choose, out of the reading from Isaiah, the line which most appeals to you. Dominic, would you read the words from Isaiah again."

This time Dominic used the Bible on the table. He again read the words Jesus had used.

> "The spirit of the Lord is on me.
> because he has anointed me
> to bring good news to the poor ..."

Ayung suddenly interrupted, "It's just not true."

"What isn't true?" asked Theresa.

"This 'good news for the poor'. There's no good news for the poor. It's just a load of nonsense."

There was a gasp from the others.

"What do you mean, it's nonsense?" Nancy asked. "How can you say such a thing? Don't you believe that what the Bible says is true? And I really thought you were a Christian!"

Nancy seemed almost to be in tears.

Ayung went on, "Yesterday I had no food in the house. A neighbour gave me just a little rice and that was all I had to feed my children. How can you talk about good news?"

Then they realised that Ayung was doing exactly what Dominic had asked. He was pretending to be one of the very poor women in Theresa's group.

Theresa thought desperately. This was exactly what she feared might happen in her group if she started to introduce anything Christian. How could she answer Ayung?

"How many agree with Ayung?" she asked.

Matthew hesitantly raised his hand while Solomon put his right up.

"I am speaking for myself now," said Solomon. "I was trying to imagine what those words, 'good news to the poor', would mean to someone desperately poor. If there's not enough food in the house for your children's evening meal, what is good news? Surely someone putting a food parcel on your doorstep, but that doesn't happen."

"It can do," said Margaret. "My family were desperately poor in Scotland. During the war there was often very little food in the house. But Mother was a woman of very great faith and simply asked God for help. And always something turned up. And we made up for it in other ways. We were a very happy family and two of us at least learnt to rely very much on God. That's why I became a minister."

"You mean you lived in the U.K. and you were poor?" asked Nancy.

"Yes," said Margaret. "In those days some were very poor. There are still poor people in the U.K. but it's not as bad as here. People in the U.K. at least have enough food to eat though some may not have very good living conditions."

Theresa had been thinking hard and now knew what her answer should be.

"I was in the same position when I was expecting Benedict," she said. "I had nothing, not even faith anymore. But I prayed. I had been taught about Jesus at school so I simply asked, 'Jesus, if you are really there, please help me.' Then, as I was walking down a street wondering where to go, a woman looked at me and said, 'You look as if you need some help. Would you like to come with me?' She was a Christian. She took me into her home. Her church really did care for me right through my pregnancy and afterwards. I can't prove that what Jesus said will be true for everyone, but it was certainly true for me. Does that help to answer your question, Ayung?"

Ayung nodded slowly.

"Let's look at the passage a bit more," said Theresa. "Did anything else seem to say anything to you?"

"The line that appealed to me," said Solomon, "was the one about 'freedom for prisoners'. I don't think Jesus meant he was going to let bad characters out of jail although I have known men who have become Christians while in prison. I think he meant two things: Freedom for those who are imprisoned by circumstances. Like some of your families in the shanty town who simply cannot find a way to a better life. And then freedom for those who are prisoners or slaves to bad habits or wrong ways of thinking. I know of people who have turned to Jesus and found that kind of freedom. I can think of at least three people who have turned to Jesus and been healed of their craving. But what if the person doesn't really believe? Can such a person find release?"

"No!" said Nancy. "The person has got to believe first."

"But if other people are praying?"

"They still have to turn to Jesus," said Nancy. "We're saved by faith in Christ Jesus."

"But surely," said Margaret, "a person who is in that kind of prison can't really help himself or herself. It must be through the prayers of others. I think a prayer of faith, especially by a group of people, will really bring release. Perhaps not straight away but in God's time. Had you someone in mind, Solomon?"

Solomon hesitated for a moment.

"Yes," he said, "my youngest son."

Solomon went on to explain how his son had left home and how worried he and his wife were.

Again Theresa wondered what she should do. She wanted to get on with the lesson. At the same time she realised that when you lead a Bible study, people's own problems might well be raised. That was one of the things a Bible study was about.

"I think," she said, "that when we come to our time of

prayer, we should pray for Solomon's son. But what about the rest of you? Did any other line strike anyone as being important?"

Theresa let the discussion continue for about ten minutes and then said, "Now I want to look for a short time at the whole story. What do you think is the most important lesson of the story? And is there a lesson we can act upon? Something that you feel we should do as a result of reading the passage? I don't want to discuss this; I just want you to give a simple answer.

Margaret said, "I think the key lesson is that Jesus was really on the side of the poor and the oppressed. As Christians, we should follow his example."

"I've been wondering about that," said Solomon. "I have people in my congregation who are quite high up in Government. I might be able to persuade them to take an interest in the conditions some of your people are living in. Perhaps they can get things moving for you."

Theresa could hardly believe this. Just when she was becoming really depressed at the lack of progress, here was an offer of help. And it had come because of the Bible study she and Dominic had led.

"That would be wonderful," she said.

Solomon went on, "Give me a couple of weeks to think about it and talk to some people. Then we can have a meeting."

Ayung said, "What struck me, and I'm speaking for myself now, was that Jesus was determined to stick to his message whatever the cost. They tried to kill him. He faced tremendous opposition not just on this occasion but right through to the cross. And in the end, the resurrection gave him the victory when it seemed that all was lost. It is telling me to persevere with what I believe to be right."

No one seemed to want to add anything to this so Theresa decided to conclude her lesson.

"Thank you, Ayung. That's what struck me when I read the passage with Dominic. I do get very discouraged at times but I realised I must persevere, whatever the difficulties. Jesus didn't give up so I shouldn't give up. And now Solomon has given me fresh hope. Thank you for all your comments. To end our lesson, I am going to hand over to Dominic."

Dominic carried on, "I think it would help us if we tried to learn those words from Isaiah. You probably know them already but let's say them again. I'll read them and then we'll say them together.

> "The Spirit of the Lord is on me,
> because he has anointed me
> to preach good news to the poor.
> He sent me to proclaim freedom for the prisoners
> and recovery of sight for the blind,
> to release the oppressed,
> to proclaim the year of the Lord's favour."

When they had done this, Dominic went back to his seat and Matthew came forward.

"Thank you, Theresa and Dominic," he said.

Much to their surprise, the rest of the class clapped them!

Matthew continued, "Now I want you to think of the lesson and the lesson plan. What struck you as being really good? And was there anything that could be improved? What do you think?"

Solomon was the first to speak. "I think it was a very good Bible study."

"It was different from many Bible studies I've been to," said Ayung. "Most of the leaders start with a bit of discussion but then just lecture the group and everyone falls asleep after about half an hour. You made sure we all had the opportunity to say something. I thought that was very good."

"The way you tried to describe the synagogue with just a few simple things was good," said Margaret. "The scroll must have taken quite a time to make."

"Yes," said Theresa, "Dominic gave me the paper and glue.

I wasn't sure whether it was right to make one as not everyone can get hold of writing materials. But Dominic can keep it and use it again for one of his classes. It won't be wasted."

"Was there anything in the lesson that could have been improved or changed?" asked Matthew.

"You didn't explain what 'the year of the Lord's favour' meant," said Nancy. "But perhaps it would have been too much for your class to understand."

"We thought about that," replied Theresa. "But I had so many things to explain - the synagogue and the meaning of the Naaman bit. I thought that was as much as my group could take. I would have explained it if someone had asked."

"It is a good point, Nancy," said Matthew. "But you have to think about how much information your group can take in during one lesson. I think Theresa got it about right on this occasion. Any other comments?"

No one answered so Matthew continued, "Well, we've come to our prayer time. Don't let's forget Solomon's son. Solomon, what is your son's name?"

"Thomas," replied Solomon. "Thank you for remembering him."

Lessons to learn from this chapter

1. If you are leading a Bible study, make sure you involve the people in the group. Give everyone the opportunity to speak but don't put pressure on people – if they just want to listen, that's fine.

2. It is important to make Bible studies interesting. Theresa did this by:
   (a) Having two readers who read dramatically in a way that brought out the meaning.
   (b) Acting out the story, in this case using the scroll.
   (c) Explaining the context.
   (d) Getting people involved using imagination and discussion.

3. Know the capability and attitudes of your group (e.g. not all of Theresa's class can read and not all are Christians.)

4. Theresa's and Dominic's lesson is an example of 'team teaching' - two or three teachers working together. Such lessons can be very effective but must be planned carefully so that each person knows when to speak and what to do.

NOTE: See Appendix D for Theresa's and Dominic's lesson plan.

Chapter 14

Trouble at home for Nancy – different kinds of learning

It was Nancy's turn to feel upset as she got the bus to take her to Matthew's house for the next lesson. She felt sick as she went over and over in her mind what had happened that weekend. Her youngest son was sixteen years old and had always gone with her to church. This Sunday he had told her that he would not be coming. His friends had invited him to go to a motor racing meeting.

Nancy had argued with him. She had told him that God should come first but he had told her he was old enough to please himself. He added that as Dad never went to church, he didn't see why he should go every Sunday. They had ended by shouting at each other. But he had still gone to the race!

Nancy and her son were now speaking to each other but tension was very high. Nancy was dreading the next Sunday when he would probably say he was not going to church again.

What would the church think of her now? She was supposed to be an evangelist but couldn't keep her own family faithful. She would lose face. Worse still, her own son would start down the slippery path that could lead to losing his faith in Jesus.

When she reached Matthew's house, she could hardly reply to the others when they greeted her. Margaret immediately sensed there was something wrong. She asked Nancy if she was alright. Nancy snapped back that of course she was alright. Matthew began his lesson.

"Do you remember," he asked, "a lesson we had some time ago about different ways of teaching?"

"Yes," said Dominic. "I remember it clearly because I couldn't think of any teaching methods to start with."

"Towards the end of that lesson," Matthew continued, "I gave a short talk about why we should use different methods. Can any of you remember some of the reasons?"

Ayung replied, "To keep students interested."

"To help those who learn in different ways," said Solomon.

"I remember you said people remember over three quarters of what they do but only about a quarter of what they hear," said Theresa.

"Excellent," said Matthew. You must have been doing your homework well. But there was another reason I gave which I didn't explain at the time."

"You said something about driving a car," said Dominic. "I remembered that because I was wondering if I could afford to take driving lessons. Was it about actually doing something?"

"You're on the right lines," said Matthew. "In this lesson, I am going to talk about different kinds of learning. They are called 'Learning Domains'. And I am going to make it simple by thinking of only four different kinds of learning. If you want to learn more, there are books you can read."

Matthew went to his battered blackboard and wrote down the heading and then four letters. Underneath, he wrote what the letters stood for.

DIFFERENT KINDS OF LEARNING
(Learning Domains)

M U D A

MEMORY
UNDERSTANDING
DOING
ATTITUDE

Matthew continued, "First, let's think about Memory. Often, when you teach, you want people to remember things. For example, if you are teaching people to speak a different language, they have to remember new words and what they mean. Then they have to remember how to make up sentences."

"It's like that when you are teaching people to read and write," said Theresa. "First of all, they have to remember how to write the letters of the alphabet."

"That's right," said Matthew. "Remembering is a very important part of learning. Let's think about that a bit more. Dominic, you and Theresa used the way of learning which I am calling '**MEMORY**' twice in your lesson last week. Can you think of one of the times?"

"Yes," said Dominic. "We wanted to end the Bible study with something which summed up the lesson. Also, we wanted to give people something to remember. We hoped it would help them and comfort them when times were difficult.

"We chose the key verses:

>'The Spirit of the Lord is on me,
>because he has anointed me
>to preach good news to the poor ...'

You know the rest."

"It worked," said Theresa. "I used the lesson in my group

yesterday and it went very well. We repeated the verse about four times and then one of the women who has a real gift for music started to sing it. That made it even easier to remember. I'm sure they won't forget that verse."

"That's right," said Matthew. "A verse or text to remember can be very valuable to a person long after they have forgotten the actual lesson. I can still remember verses I learnt as a child and they are a great help to me."

"Many old people," said Solomon, "find comfort in verses they learnt in their early years. 'The Lord is my Shepherd' is a favourite but there are many others."

"Learning by heart can be a very helpful area of learning," said Matthew. "And when you think about what people remember, you find that memory is a very important part of the learning process. It is part of life itself. But, Theresa, you and Dominic used memory in another part of your lesson. Can you think how?"

"I got the people to imagine the scene," said Theresa. "That was because we didn't have Bibles and not all the group could read either."

"Did it work?" said Matthew.

"Yes," said Theresa. "Three or four came to me afterwards and said what a vivid picture they had of the story. I suppose I hadn't realised I was helping them to remember the story for such a long time after the lesson."

"So we have two different ways of teaching which will help people to remember things from our lesson. The first is repeating things until people know them by heart. The second is by reading or telling the story in a very dramatic way. You could make a small play out of the story, or maybe mime the story as it is being read."

"There is another way. You have used it in this lesson," said Ayung. "You have written four letters. They make a strange word, MUDA, but it is one that can be remembered quite easily."

"Yes," said Matthew, "you can often find first letters of

words which make a list and that helps people to remember. Sometimes it is possible to make little rhymes, for example:

'Matthew, Mark, Luke and John
Acts and Romans follow on.'

This is a good rhyme to help beginners who are studying the Bible to remember the order of the first books of the New Testament. Another example, if you are using an English translation of the Bible, is a way of helping to remember the order of four of St. Paul's letters: Galatians, Ephesians, Philippians and Colossians. The vowels in the names follow the order of the vowels in the English alphabet: 'a', Galatians; 'e', Ephesians, and so on.

To sum up, try to find ways of helping students to remember key things in your teaching. 'Remembering' is one part of learning. Now let's look at the second letter, 'U' - **UNDERSTANDING**."

"I think that is the most important part of learning," said Solomon. "But I am not sure if I know what it really means to 'understand' something. It's something you feel in yourself, but how does it come about?"

"There have been many books written about understanding," answered Matthew. "But you're right. It is very hard to explain. At the same time, most of us know in ourselves what it means. We all have had the experience of learning something new and being able to say 'Oh yes! I see it now'. Most of the teaching methods we have learnt about will help people to understand. But there are some which are not helpful. Can you think of any?"

"Learning a passage by heart unless it has already been explained," said Theresa.

"Giving a boring lecture," suggested Nancy. "I know some lectures can be very good and helpful, but it's no good just sending people to sleep."

Margaret spoke. "I think understanding is a bit like building a house. You've got to start with the foundations. Then you build the walls. Each piece must be connected to the last one.

And you can't put on the roof until you've got the walls. So it is with understanding. You've got to add to what you already know. You can't just put in an entirely new piece of knowledge unless it connects in your brain with what is already there.

"I once had a student who thought a girl he knew was possessed by demons. In fact, the girl was suffering from depression after the birth of her child. The student had never learnt that there was an illness called depression. He didn't know that some mothers can get very depressed after having a child. So he was not able to understand what was happening. He wanted to cast out the demons, when in fact there were no demons there. The girl needed to see a good doctor or to be prayed for by someone who understood what kind of prayer to use."

"Thank you," said Matthew. "I think Margaret's comparison with building a house a very good one. There is, however, another side to understanding which I will just mention. It doesn't happen very often. Sometimes a person can make a real jump in his or her mind. Some of the very great scientists or painters have done this. They have seen in their minds something which to most people would be completely new. A good expression for this is 'The light has dawned'. But this doesn't happen very often.

"Almost all teaching methods help a person to understand, but the best of all is to get a person to do something in connection with the lesson. It may be something practical. When you all taught mini-lessons right at the start of the course, I am sure that helped you to understand how to plan a lesson much more than if I had just talked about it. Another important thing in helping students to understand is to give them time to ask questions. And if a person does ask a question, even if it is a very simple one, always try to give a clear answer. Do all you can to encourage students to ask questions. And never, ever tell them that the question is simple or that the answer is obvious.

"As I have said, I do like the comparison with building a

house. Start with what people know and build up knowledge from that. It's a very good illustration. Now let's think about the next different kind of learning or 'Learning Domain'. That is 'D' for **DOING**. We all need to learn how to do things even if it is just how to cook, or how to drive a car."

"Is there much 'doing' in learning about the Bible or holding a church meeting?" asked Ayung.

"Of course," said Nancy. "You need a lot of practical skills. For example, if you are reading a lesson in a church, you need to know how to project your voice so that everyone can hear you. You need to be able to read in a way that holds people's attention."

"Taking services involves a lot of 'doing' skills," said Solomon. "We always teach people who are learning to be priests to speak clearly. We teach them how to celebrate Holy Communion. We even have to teach some of them how to walk in public, otherwise they would just shuffle along."

"Also leading meetings needs a lot of skill," added Margaret. "We all know about meetings where the chairperson allows people to talk on and on. It wastes everyone's time."

"So what teaching methods would be helpful in teaching people how to 'do' things properly?" asked Matthew.

"Demonstration," said Ayung.

"Practice. And observing others, for example fellow students," suggested Solomon. "Also discussion of their strengths and weaknesses when they are reading or preaching a sermon."

"If you can get hold of a CD player that will record, it can help students to listen to themselves. A camcorder is even better as they see themselves as well," said Margaret.

"I wish every teacher or minister could listen to themselves once a year," said Matthew. "They can spot any mistakes they are making. Personally I ask my wife to let me know if I am picking up bad habits when I preach a sermon in my church. She's very good at telling me where I go wrong. But let's think of other kinds of learning where 'doing' skills are important."

"I had to go to some 'First Aid' classes," said Dominic. "We learnt some theory, but most important was how to treat simple injuries. The teacher demonstrated what to do and then we had to practise what he taught us. We also learnt how to deal with a person who had a heart attack. I had to practise it six times before I got it right but I still remember what to do."

"That's a very useful 'Doing' skill," said Margaret. "But I hope you won't have to demonstrate it in this class!"

"There are many skills which you have to learn by simply 'doing' them," said Solomon. "The teacher can teach by giving a demonstration, but the pupil has to actually do the work in order to learn. Remember again that Jesus learnt to be a carpenter by actually making things."

"That's a wonderful example," said Matthew. "Jesus watched his father, the master carpenter, and then made things himself. But now, let me change the subject. Let's think about the hardest of all, 'A' for **ATTITUDES**."

"What do you mean by 'attitudes'?" asked Dominic.

"An attitude is something a person thinks or feels very strongly and deeply about," said Margaret "Attitudes can develop from childhood. Or they can be put into a person's mind by wrong ways of teaching."

"You mean like the man in my group who was convinced that Jesus was going to come again very soon," said Dominic.

"Or the people who were very frightened of the medicine man in my group," said Ayung. "It would be very hard to change that kind of attitude."

"That's exactly right," said Matthew. "But should a teacher try to change peoples' attitudes?"

"No, he has no right to do that," said Nancy.

"I don't agree," said Theresa. "I spend most of my time trying to change attitudes. The poor people don't think they have any power. The Government think the poor are lazy and don't deserve help. You've got to change attitudes!"

"But how do you know that your own attitudes are right?" said Solomon. "It's very easy for a teacher to have attitudes.

Even teachers can have ways of thinking that they will not change. Some teachers teach children to become suicide bombers. That is horribly wrong, but such teachers will not change their attitudes."

"Surely the Bible says that God cares for the poor. So we should care as well," Theresa replied.

"So you check your attitudes from the Bible?" Matthew asked.

"Well, some of them," said Theresa.

"How do you know that attitudes in the Bible are always right?" asked Margaret.

"Of course the Bible's right," said Nancy. "It's the word of God."

"I find that hard," said Ayung. "I don't think the world was created in six days and yet that's what the Bible says. Do we believe the Bible or do we believe the scientists?"

"The Bible's right," snapped Nancy. "It's God's word and you've got to believe it."

Matthew asked gently, "Would anything make you think in a different way?"

"No it would not. That's the trouble with people today. They question this and that. They never really believe. I don't care what people say, I won't change."

Nancy was in tears.

Margaret went up to Nancy and put her arms around her. By now Nancy was crying. Matthew was deeply disturbed. He knew some parts of his course might arouse deep emotions, but he hadn't expected this. And it had come right at the end of the lesson. Some of the others looked very uncomfortable. Matthew wondered if he ought to end the session, but that would mean sending them away with the emotions unresolved. Something had to be done, but what?

"Let's stop and have a break," he suggested. "I'll ask my wife to get some drinks. Then we'll talk about this just a little more, have a time of prayer and think about it again when we're fresh."

While they were drinking their tea, Margaret and Nancy talked quietly. Nancy found herself pouring out her problems about her son. She also felt very guilty because, although she was an evangelist, she hadn't converted her husband.

As she talked, Margaret realised that it was probably because of her very rigid attitude that her husband had remained an outsider and her son was rebelling. "A change of attitude is needed," thought Margaret, as Nancy poured out her anger against those who didn't really believe the Bible. "And yet," thought Margaret, "she is right in one way. The Bible is our authority. It does tell us what to believe, and God speaks to us through the Bible. It's just that Nancy is making it into a book of rules. Also she wouldn't be such a good evangelist if she didn't have strong feelings." As she thought about this, Margaret realised that continuing the lesson would only upset Nancy more. She arranged with Nancy that she would go to see her outside of the class.

"I think," Margaret said to the group, "that we should leave the topic of 'attitudes' to another time. It's nearly time for prayer and we can finish Mathew's lesson next week. Would that be alright, Matthew?"

"Of course," Matthew said.

"Matthew, don't you have some work to set? Perhaps it would be a good time to do that now," suggested Ayung.

"Yes," replied Matthew. "It's a very simple task but you need time to prepare. Theresa and Dominic have already given us their lesson. I want the rest of you to prepare a lesson for us. I'd like you, Margaret, to work with Ayung. And would you, Solomon, work with Nancy? Wait until Nancy feels better before you discuss what to teach. I want you to plan a lesson and teach it to us. You can choose a topic, but it must be a lesson that you can actually teach to your own students. There is plenty of time. We have two more lessons to go before Margaret and Ayung give their lesson. Is that alright?"

The three of them; Solomon, Ayung and Margaret, answered approvingly and Nancy managed to nod her head.

"Good," said Matthew, "Now we've come to our prayer time. If you don't mind, I'll lead it myself. I am going to lead a meditation which may be a help to Nancy and to all of us. I have certainly found it very helpful myself. And instead of praying aloud, there will be a chance for silent prayer in the meditation. So let's relax and remember God's presence with us."

Lessons to learn from this chapter

1. There are different kinds of learning. These are called 'Learning Domains'.

2. Four of these domains are:
   Memory
   Understanding
   Doing
   Attitude

Attitude means how a person thinks or feels about something. Often people feel very strongly about something or some way of doing things and simply cannot change the way they think. Racial prejudice is an example.

3. Different kinds of learning may need different teaching methods.

4. If someone in the group shows deep emotion, either:
   (a) deal with it very sympathetically in the lesson
or
   (b) break off or gently go on to a different subject. Make sure the person has an opportunity to talk to someone during the lesson or immediately after it.

Chapter 15

Matthew leads a meditation

Matthew began, "Before I start this meditation, I want you to sit in a relaxed position. One of the best ways is to sit upright, hands on knees, with palms open and eyes closed in order to use your imagination more easily. But sit in whatever way is most comfortable for you. Now I am going to read the passage I want you to think about. Then I will ask you to imagine the scene as clearly as you can. If you have not got a good imagination, just think of the words in the story. Let the words of Jesus sink into your heart. The passage comes from St. Mark's Gospel, Chapter Four."

Matthew paused for a moment and then read the story.

"On that day, when evening had come, Jesus said to the disciples, 'Let us go across to the other side of the lake.' And leaving the crowd behind, they took him with them in the boat just as he was. Other boats were with him. A great gale arose, and the waves beat into the boat, so that the boat was already being swamped. But he was in the stern, asleep on the cushion; and they woke him up and said to him, 'Teacher, do you not care that we are perishing?' He woke up and rebuked the wind and said to the sea, 'Peace! Be still!' Then the wind ceased and there was a dead calm. He said to them, 'Why are you afraid? Have you still no faith?' And they were filled with great awe and said to one another, 'Who then is this, that even the wind and the sea obey him?'"

Matthew continued speaking slowly and with pauses to give the class time to think.

"Try to picture the scene. If possible, put yourself in the story. Try to imagine that you are one of the disciples in the boat. Think of yourself as Thomas or Andrew or one of the others. If you can't do that, then just picture in your mind the group of disciples or concentrate on the words of the disciples and Jesus.

"Jesus is at the edge of the Lake, the Sea of Galilee, and there are crowds of people around him… He turns to his disciples and says to them, 'Let us go across to the other side.' Picture yourself and the others getting into the boat and pushing off… You and the others row out into the lake and hoist a sail."

Matthew paused to give them time to make a picture in their minds before he continued.

"You are in the middle of the Lake now. Jesus is asleep in the stern, his head resting on a cushion. He is so tired after a very long day with the crowds… Then the wind starts to grow stronger, the water gets rougher."

Matthew started to speak more quickly, with a sense of urgency in his voice, "Soon, there is a gale blowing down from the mountains to the north… The waves grow higher and water begins to pour over the side into the boat… You try to empty the water out with a pot, but it swirls into the bottom of the boat which is tossing and turning… It's a long way to land now and the water is very deep."

Matthew again paused.

"You shout to the others, 'The boat's going to sink, we're going to drown. What can we do?'... One of them replies, 'We must wake the Master. He'll know what to.' You stagger to the stern and there is Jesus still asleep... 'How can he sleep through this?' you wonder. You shake him, 'Master, Master, wake up! Don't you care if we all drown?'"

Again, Matthew paused to let the scene sink into their minds.

"Jesus opens his eyes and becomes aware of the boat tossing and rolling in the rough sea. You help him to his feet... Jesus looks up to heaven and in a loud voice says, 'Peace! Be still!'"

Matthew paused again to let the scene sink deep into their minds and then continued with an expression of amazement in his voice, "And the wind suddenly dies down. The sea becomes smooth and the boat stops rolling... There is a dead calm. Then Jesus turns to you and the others with a disappointed and yet deeply caring look in his eyes. He says to you, 'Have you still no faith?'"

This time after a longer pause, Matthew went on, "Now I want you to apply this passage to yourself or to someone you know. I want you to think now of anything that is deeply troubling you. If there is nothing troubling you just at the moment, think of a friend. Maybe you have a friend who has a really big problem facing him or her. That trouble is like the storm. We each have to go through quite big storms in life. Think of the storm you or your friend is going through."

Matthew paused for a minute or so, to give his class time to think about this.

"Now think of yourself kneeling in front of Jesus. Try to imagine Jesus standing in front of you. Think of the storm you are going through.

"Now hear Jesus saying to you, 'Peace! Be still!' If you are thinking of a friend who is going through a storm in life, imagine Jesus saying to that friend, 'Peace, be still.' Jesus says to you, or your friend, 'Peace, be still!' 'Peace, be still!'"

Matthew let the silence last for about a minute and again, very quietly, said, "Peace! Be still!"

He again paused in silence.

"Now," said Matthew, "I am going to end this time of thinking, of meditation, with a prayer.

"Lord Jesus, let your peace sink deeply into our hearts and minds. Let your peace be in the hearts and minds of those we love. Help us to remember that you are always with us, whatever problems we have to face. Thank you, Lord, for your love and care. Amen."

It was some time before anyone spoke, then Margaret broke the silence.

"Thank you, Matthew, for that. It was a great help to me."

"Me too," said Theresa. "In the last part, I thought of a friend in one of my groups who is deeply troubled. I do hope she finds some peace and help."

"I'm sure she will," said Solomon. "I was thinking of my son and Jesus saying to him, 'Peace!' and suddenly, almost like a voice, it came to me, 'Don't worry about him anymore. He is alright.'"

"I found it easy to imagine the storm," said Ayung. "I've been in storms on the sea, although not quite so bad that I was afraid I would drown. But I could imagine what the disciples were feeling. And I liked the idea of thinking about the storms in our own lives. That was very helpful."

They got up to go to the door. As they were leaving, Margaret spoke to Nancy.

"How are you feeling?" she asked.

"Still upset inside," said Nancy. "Matthew wants me to have faith but I don't feel I have much faith just now."

"Look," said Margaret, "You said I could come and see you so we could have more time to talk. How about the day after tomorrow?"

She and Nancy fixed a time and Margaret felt quite relieved

that Nancy had agreed to talk. After Nancy had gone, Matthew asked Margaret if there was anything he could do.

"I don't think so," answered Margaret. "She really does need to loosen up a bit, but that is going to be very hard. I'll try to get to the root of the problem when I see her. But I'm sure it's because she's so dogmatic that her husband keeps his distance from Christianity. If only she could be a bit more relaxed it would help them both."

"Let me know how you get on," said Matthew. "I'll have to talk again about attitudes but it might be good to leave it for a week or two. I'll see you at college tomorrow."

Lessons to learn from this chapter

1. This is one way of leading a meditation. Don't use it every time as some people find it hard to imagine stories. For those who have a good imagination, it is a very powerful way of prayer.

2. It is often good, when tensions run high, to stop everything and turn to prayer. Try to let God into the situation. But remember that when a person is really upset, that person cannot always pray. The person may feel that God is far away.

3. Never let a person who is upset leave without the hope of some kind of help. They must be sure that someone cares enough to help them through their problems. But beware of people who come to you constantly with problems. Some people do play on the sympathy of a teacher. If this happens, you must set clear guidelines.

For example, say, "Come and see me at such and such a time. I've got half an hour to spare then." You are concerned and willing to help but you have other calls on your time as well.

4. It could be that another member of the group can help. It need not always be the leader.

Chapter 16

Changing peoples' attitudes (i.e. set ways of thinking)

Before the lesson, Matthew had a discussion with Margaret about Nancy. The problem was that in this lesson he was going to talk about attitudes. By attitudes he meant 'the way people think and feel about others' or, 'the way people think and feel about ideas and beliefs'.

For Nancy, the way she felt about the Bible and her belief that it was the infallible word of God, every word coming directly from God; all this added up to her attitude to the Bible. It was an attitude which was rooted deeply in her upbringing and personality. But behind the attitude were other things. She was afraid of having a deeply held belief challenged or altered in any way. This fear brought back fears she had from her childhood, which had been a very hard one. Her mother had died when she was very young and this had led to deep feelings of insecurity in herself. Often the attitudes people have are a deep part of their character.

Some attitudes can be very good. For example, the way people of many races feel that they have a duty to welcome strangers into their homes is good. But to refuse to be hospitable towards a person because that person belongs to a different tribe or race is a wrong attitude. Jesus tried to break down this wrong attitude in his parable of the Good Samaritan. And part of a teacher's job is to try and change wrong attitudes. In his lesson, Matthew wanted to show what kind of teaching would help to change people's attitudes. But was it safe to discuss this when Nancy was in such an emotional state?

Margaret had been to see Nancy.

"I had a long talk with Nancy," she said, "and I told her that the next lesson would be about attitudes. I asked her if she could face such a lesson. I said you would be very gentle and all of us, not only her, would learn a lot from the lesson.

"Nancy said she would be alright but that she wasn't going to change. I think you should go ahead. If she sees that one or two of us have changed our attitudes to a deeply held principle then that might help her. At the moment she feels she is the only one who is sticking up for her principles. But she has to learn that if you are going to be a good teacher, you must know and accept what is inside yourself."

When all the students had arrived, with Nancy rather tight-lipped and looking very nervous, Matthew started.

"Last week we looked at three 'learning domains'. That is, three different kinds of learning. Can you remember what they were?"

"Knowing," said Theresa.

"Doing skills," added Ayung.

"Remembering," said Dominic.

"Good," said Matthew. "But there was one kind of learning which we didn't consider. That is 'attitude'."

Matthew wrote on the board:

ATTITUDE

He continued, "By 'attitude', I mean the way we think and

feel about deeply held beliefs or principles. Or the way we think about other people. A very common bad attitude is racial prejudice.

"Let me give an example from my teaching as a lecturer at the college which I think you will understand. I have a class in college of about twenty students. They are new students and they want me to give them a lecture each time I teach. They like to take notes so that they can learn the facts by heart. Then, when they go into the examination room, they will be able to write down what they have learnt. It doesn't really matter what the question says. They will just write down things they have learnt from their notes.

"Now I have been trying to get them to think for themselves. I have used other ways of teaching. I have done this because some of the students are not good at understanding lectures. Also I do not think real learning is copying down the ideas of other people, even when the ideas come from a famous professor like me."

They all laughed at this.

"So two weeks ago," Matthew continued, "some of the brightest students went to the college Principal and complained about my teaching. What should I do about the situation?"

There was an uncomfortable silence.

Dominic blushed!

"I thought exactly the same thing," he said. "I liked you but I didn't think you were a good teacher. I was so accustomed to teachers giving lectures. But I realise now I was wrong. My attitude to teaching has changed."

"I thought the same," said Solomon. "I think I told you that I nearly left the course after the second lesson. And after my talk with the Bishop I came back determined to prove I was right and that the course was a waste of time."

"Do you still think you were right?" asked Ayung.

"No," said Solomon. "I've come to see that Matthew is a very good teacher. I have learnt a huge amount. But you see, like Dominic, it was my attitude to teaching that was wrong."

"So you changed your attitude?" asked Nancy.

"Yes, and I think I was right to change. But it wasn't easy. My own education, that is the time I was at college, and also the way my Father had been educated, made me think there was only one way of teaching. It was very hard to change. In fact, if the Bishop hadn't told me to carry on, I wouldn't have changed."

"So what can Matthew do about his class of students?" asked Margaret. "If his students don't have confidence in him, they won't learn much."

"Does the Principal support you?" asked Dominic.

"Yes," said Matthew. "It would be a disaster if he didn't. If he insisted that I taught in the traditional way, I think I would have to leave the college.

"I must admit, however, that I didn't always think the same way myself. I used to give lectures like most of the others until I realised I wasn't helping some of the students to learn. Those who learnt best from lectures passed the examinations well. Most of the others did pass but with low marks. Now that I use a variety of teaching methods, including lectures from time to time, all the students are doing better."

"Can't you use your results to prove you are right?" asked Nancy. "If you showed the students who are complaining that you get good results, surely that would convince them?"

"Also," said Dominic, "after we criticised you, in the very next lesson you did something to convince us that your methods were good. I can remember this very clearly.

"You didn't try to cover up what we were thinking. You faced our criticisms and made us think more deeply about them. And you gave us a very good lesson which showed that we could learn a huge amount from the new methods of teaching. Couldn't you do the same with your college students? At the end of your lesson, show them that they have learnt a lot and can remember it."

"I agree," said Margaret. "But I think you and the Principal should do more. I think that together you should face the whole class and give them clear reasons why you are using different teaching methods."

"I wonder," said Ayung, "if you could fit some teaching about adult education into your ordinary lessons. Every priest or minister has to do some teaching. Could you have ten minutes at the end of the lesson to discuss the ways of teaching you have used? And show them how those ways of teaching have helped them to learn."

"The problem," said Theresa, "is that our attitudes are so much a part of us. Solomon, you had to unlearn what you had experienced over many years. I think you were wonderful the way you did change your ideas. And I have had to change my attitude towards you. I thought you were very stuffy at the beginning but I was quite wrong. I suppose that was partly because of my attitude to my own father and 'father figures'."

They all laughed at this.

"Thank you for being so honest," said Matthew. "The Principal and I have worked out a strategy to answer the students' criticisms. It is very much along the lines you suggest. We are going to have a talk with the students and we're going to show them the examination results of last year's classes. Fortunately these were very good. Also I am going to give a brief talk about why I use different teaching methods. But I think your suggestion, Ayung, that I include a short time in each lesson about how to teach adults is a very interesting one. As you say, my college students all have to teach adults as part of their ministry."

"But now, let's change the subject a little. I want each of you to think of attitudes in your own church, in your community or in yourself, which you think should be changed. I'll give you five minutes to jot this down on your notepads."

They thought hard and during the five minutes each of them wrote down two or three things. They had no difficulty doing this!

"Just one each and be very brief," said Matthew. "Who will

start?"

Ayung started, "Some villagers feel they have to placate the spirits, even if it means sacrificing a valuable animal."

"People of my race still look down on the lower classes or castes," said Solomon. "Even in my congregation, a few of the higher caste people think poorest castes deserve what they get. I can't persuade them it is not true."

"Some of the Chinese are like," said Nancy. "They despise those who are of mixed race. The white Chinese are considered the best. Times are changing, but many still have that attitude."

"Some of my tribe won't help people of other tribes," said Dominic. "And some object when they see a person of a different tribe getting promoted. They try to stop the promotion going through. I used to think that way. I thought my tribe was better than the others. But since I became a Christian, I've learnt to see everyone as a brother or sister."

Margaret added her suggestion. "I have spent quite a lot of time trying to get equal rights for women. Even in England, women are often paid less than men. In some countries women are really oppressed. There is no equality at all between women and men. Many men look down on women. It's a very wrong attitude that is very hard to change."

"A quite different attitude," said Nancy, "is to do with worship in the church. There's a lot of conflict between those who want the 'old-fashioned', more traditional, worship and those who like new music and modern services. I get very worried about young people who are attracted to Christianity. When they go to a church, they find very traditional worship. This puts them off the church altogether."

"I have come up against a terrible attitude in my community," said Theresa. "When people knew I was going to have a baby, they simply ignored me. My father threw me out of the house because I had brought the family into such disgrace. I know I was a foolish teenager, but I needed help, not condemnation. But now I am bringing up Benedict, my son, I realise that at least one of my father's attitudes was right.

Benedict does need stability in his home life. I suppose my community were trying to protect that to some extent."

"Thank you again," said Matthew. "But now we come to the important part of the lesson so far as we teachers are concerned. What teaching methods can we use to change attitudes?"

"Thinking of Nancy's point," said Margaret, "I've tried preaching many times about the need to bring services up-to-date. I have pleaded with people to include modern hymns and to use language people can understand. But in the congregation back home, many listened politely and took no notice! Some of the people were very good and were enthusiastic about making changes. But some just refused to change at all. The sermons were not much good."

"I have found," said Solomon, "that preaching often doesn't change people's attitudes. My congregation is the same as the one you had. Those who have open minds do take notice but a lot have closed minds. For those, even good sermons make no difference to the way they think."

"Preaching and lecturing are very similar," said Matthew. "Lectures can change the attitudes of people who have open minds. But for those who don't want to change, a lecture rarely helps."

"I think discussion and listening to other people's points of view helps to change attitudes," said Ayung. "It has helped me."

"How about role play?" asked Theresa. "If you put yourself in the other person's place and pretend to be him or her, you begin to see what it is like for that person."

"A field visit could be useful," said Margaret. "For example, visiting a different community and listening to their problems might change people's attitudes about other races. Or perhaps a group from another community could come and speak to them."

Ayung made his contribution. "Matthew, you used what might be described as a problem or a case study when you started this lesson. You gave the example of a class that didn't agree with your teaching methods. Perhaps a case study could help to change people's attitudes."

"Good!" said Matthew. "We have four possible teaching methods we can use to help change people's attitudes. I'll write these down."

Matthew turned to his board:

TEACHING METHODS WHICH HELP TO CHANGE ATTITUDES

Role Play
Discussion
Field Visit
(or invite a group from outside to come and talk)
Case Study

"Sometimes a lecture or sermon can change attitudes, but it must be interesting and illustrated with stories. If you can tell good jokes that really helps. But on the whole, lecturing is not a good teaching method for changing attitudes."

"What do you mean by 'telling good jokes'?" asked Dominic.

"If you can put jokes into your lecture, it puts the listeners into a good humour," answered Matthew. "They listen more carefully. The jokes get the people on your side, especially if you tell them against yourself. Then you have a chance of making them think about deeply held attitudes.

"Now to sum up, I'm going to give you a short exercise. I want you to work in twos for this. I'm going to give each pair an example of a deeply ingrained attitude which should be changed. I would like you to decide what teaching methods you would use to help change the attitude.

(a) You have a group of young people in a confirmation class. They come from two different tribes which don't get on very well. This shows in the behaviour of the class. There is quite a lot of tension. You want the class to learn to work together. You want the young people to care for each other and respect each other, whatever tribe or race a person comes from.

(b) Your congregation is quite wealthy and supports a number of charities. But they are very reluctant to send any money overseas. They say, 'charity begins at home'. You feel the church should be trying to help poor people in other countries as well as your own.

(c) This is the problem suggested by Nancy. You are a minister or parish priest. Half your congregation are very traditional and want old hymns and old services. The other half, the younger ones and a few older people, want modern hymns and more up-to-date services. How do you deal with this situation?"

Theresa and Dominic discussed the first problem. They agreed that the problem of tribal loyalties was always a hard one to deal with in any country. They suggested three approaches. Dominic started off.

"First," he said, "Get the group to discuss problems which every young person has to face: problems with parents, with money, with sex and so on. It would soon become clear that whatever tribe you belonged to, you faced very similar problems. This would help to create a bond between them all."

"Next," said Theresa, "we thought a Bible study would be a good idea. We chose the parable of the Good Samaritan because the one who helps the wounded man was a person the Jews would have despised or even hated. The 'neighbour' in the parable was a member of a different tribe, a tribe disliked by the Jews. Yet he was the one who helped. And he is the one we should learn to love. We would ask the class, 'If Jesus was telling the story to you today, who would he choose to be the one who helped? It would be someone from a tribe you despised.' Then we would pray that the Holy Spirit would open their eyes to the meaning of the parable for the class today."

"Finally," said Dominic, "we would try to bring out into the open the difficulties that different tribes have in learning to love and care for each other. If possible get two adults from the different tribes who were working together to come and talk to the class. They would discuss the problems they had faced and how they found answers."

Nancy and Margaret had discussed how to help a congregation to give more to charities overseas. They felt that a good start to the problem was not to criticise but congratulate the congregation on what they gave to charity. They really were helping others by giving money. Then they would invite someone who was actually working in a foreign country to talk about conditions in that country and the good work that could be done if more money was given. Nancy and Margaret also thought that a Bible study would help, and chose the parable of the sheep and the goats (Matthew 25, 31-46). This would make clear the teaching that when we help someone in trouble, wherever they are, we are helping Jesus.

Solomon and Ayung had a much more difficult job discussing how to change people's attitudes to modern worship and hymns. They agreed that this was a problem which existed in many churches. Ayung suggested that role play was the best way of dealing with the tension. Instead of preaching a sermon they would get six members of the congregation to act out the different opinions.

"But," said Solomon, "we thought we would make it a bit different. We would ask three people who wanted modern worship to pretend to be traditionalists and put forward the traditionalist point of view! Three of those who liked traditional worship would be asked to put themselves in the place of those who wanted modern worship. The words of the discussion would be prepared beforehand by the groups, but each group could put in their own words if they felt it was right. The six members would then discuss, in front of the congregation, how they could compromise. Finally they would ask the congregation if they agreed!"

"To bring the two sides of the congregation together," said Ayung, "we would end by passing the peace, particularly with those on the opposite side, so to speak. This would help to show everyone that we are 'one body' in Jesus, whatever kind of worship we prefer."

After each group had explained their suggestions, Matthew concluded, "These plans are very good, especially as you have thought of them in such as short space of time. I think they would work and really help to change people's attitudes. But remember that this is one of the hardest parts of a teacher's job. However good your lesson, there will still be some who won't listen. Remember many people did not listen to Jesus! Even though he healed people, many of the Pharisees would not listen.

"The other point to remember is that not all attitudes you disagree with are wrong. As a teacher you must decide when it is necessary to try and change attitudes. You must be sure in your own mind that you really are helping people to grow in understanding. And my last point is that we too must all keep looking at our own deeply held attitudes. Are they Christian and should we change our way of thinking?"

Solomon had one last word to say, but it was not on the subject of 'attitudes'.

"Could I make a suggestion for the next lesson?" he asked. "I have been asked to give a lecture on the subject of the 'atonement', that is 'Why Jesus had to die on the cross'. My last attempt, at the beginning of this course, was not very successful. You said some time ago that you would give a lesson on how to give a good lecture. Do you think you could give that lesson next week? It would help me with my preparation."

"Of course," said Matthew. "So the next lesson will be 'How to give a good lecture'. Come ready to take notes!"

After the lesson, Matthew had another word with Margaret.

"I think that went quite well," he said. "Nancy was not upset again."

"No, she wasn't" said Margaret. "But you steered clear of her real problem."

"I know," said Matthew. "Her problem is very personal. Her personal problems are reflected in her attitude to the Bible and her need for security. But attitudes to the Bible really do divide Christians. Whether I should try to deal with that problem, I don't know. Maybe it would be better to leave it for a while."

Lessons to learn from this chapter

1. The hardest task a teacher has is changing people's attitudes.

2. If a teacher thinks about trying to change an attitude, he or she must be sure that the attitude to be changed is really a wrong one. A teacher can have wrong attitudes just as much as students! The teaching of Jesus is a very good guide to right and wrong attitudes.

3. Lecturing is not a good way of changing attitudes except for those students who have open minds and are willing to change. If you do use the lecture method, then tell stories and, if possible, put people at ease by making them laugh.

4. Teaching methods that are most helpful in changing attitudes are:
Role play.
Discussion (especially with people who hold different views).
Going to people who have different ways of thinking (Field Visit) or bringing outsiders to the group.
Case studies, perhaps with a common problem to solve.

5. To think about further: what is a right attitude to the question of the inspiration of the Bible?

Chapter 17

How to give a good lecture

When the group arrived for the next lesson, they still had their comfortable seats but Matthew was standing behind a reading desk. As soon as they had settled down, he described what he was going to do in the lesson.

"Last week, Solomon asked me if I would teach a lesson about 'How to give a good lecture'. He also asked me if I could give him some ideas about how to lecture on the 'Atonement'. In other words, he asked me to explain why Jesus had to die and what his death has done for us. So I am going to try and join these two topics into one lecture. So far as the Atonement is concerned, you must remember that what I say is very much my own way of interpreting the death of Jesus. Other people might give quite different lectures. But all lecturers, and preachers as well, must try to keep the attention of those who are listening. I do this by telling many stories but there are other ways, like using good pictures or visual aids.

"It does make lectures more interesting if you can use visual aids like an overhead projector or a laptop and projector. But if you do, be sure you know how to use them properly. A friend of mine once brought a laptop to help with his talk. The pictures he showed were wonderful until half way through his talk. Then the battery on the laptop failed! So he had to end his talk without any pictures. However, I am going to assume you do not have any of those gadgets. I am only going to use one very simple visual aid which you will see later in the lecture.

"One last point before I begin. When I have finished, I would like you to assess the lecture. Write down one criticism. That is one thing which you did not understand, or found boring. Then write down one good point about the lecture. In particular, tell me if you enjoyed the lecture. Enjoyment is a very important part of learning. But do be honest. If you don't find it helpful, then say so. That's all I need to say to introduce this lesson so now I am going to start my lecture. Imagine now that you are sitting in a classroom or hall listening to me talking.

"Good Morning Ladies and Gentlemen, and welcome. Today I am going to talk about two separate things. I am going to talk about some very practical points about giving a lecture. These will apply to any lecture, whatever the subject. Then I am going to try and describe how I would plan a lecture on a particular subject. The subject I have chosen is the death of Jesus. I am going to show you how I plan a lecture which explains why Jesus had to die on the cross and what his death means for us. But first, some guidance on the practical issues.

"A long time ago, I was leading a three hour service for Good Friday. I planned to give seven short talks on the seven words Jesus spoke from the cross. Between each talk there would be a time of silence, a prayer and a hymn. People could come and go during the hymn. After the first talk and during the hymn, a church official came up to me. Very politely, he told me that while I had given a very interesting talk, a lot of people couldn't hear me! I must admit I was a bit upset at first, but then I thanked him for telling me. I spoke much more loudly for the rest of the service with the result that quite a number of people told me they had found my talks helpful. But if the church official had not come to me, then all my preparation, and also the time that most people spent at the service, would have been wasted. They would not have been able to hear what I was saying!

"The first point, then, is to make sure you can be heard clearly. If you are giving a lecture in a hall or church, try and go there beforehand with a friend. Get your friend to stand at the back and listen to you. If you are using a microphone, practise with the microphone switched on. If it is not possible to practise like this then, before you start your lecture, ask your audience if they can hear you. Ask them to put their hands up if they cannot hear. There is no point in speaking at all if people cannot hear! And one other small but important thing to remember is not to drop your voice at the end of a sentence. Many people, when speaking in public, start a sentence quite loudly, but when they get to the end, they speak very quietly.

"At the same time, make sure of the opposite. Make sure you are not speaking too loudly! A friend of mine was a small man who had a very loud voice. He went to preach in a big church with a large congregation. He looked at the people and thought, 'Big church! Better speak up.' At the same time, the man in control of the microphone at the back thought, 'Small man, small voice, better turn the sound up!' The result was 'feedback', that is very loud screeching sounds, from the loudspeakers, which echoed around the building. It took about five minutes for the sound to die down. So make sure you are speaking loudly enough to be heard but not too loudly!

"The second point is to speak slowly enough for the audience to take in what they are hearing. And pause from time to time so they can make notes. Don't go too slowly as that will be boring. But many people do speak far too quickly when they are speaking to a large number of people.

"A third point is, try to look at your audience. Try to catch their eyes. It makes a great difference if people think you are speaking to them personally. This may have to come with practise. I am still, after all these years, very bad at this. I usually gaze up at the ceiling when I am speaking, which doesn't help to keep the attention of those listening.

"And finally, do make sure you can read your notes! It is best to have your lecture written out or typed on small pieces of paper which you can easily turn over." Here Matthew showed them his own notes. "If you use large sheets, then use double spacing; that is, leave a space between each line. All these points are really common sense, but it is surprising how many lecturers forget them.

"Those are some of the practical details to remember when you have to give a lecture. Now I am going to show you how I would plan a lecture. And I am taking the subject 'The Atonement' as an example.

"The first thing I do, as with lesson planning, is to work out my aim. I ask myself, 'What do I really want to tell the people who will be at the lecture?' If I am going to speak to college students, I will have to think about the kind of questions they will have to answer in their examination. I would still try to make my lecture as interesting and helpful to them as possible, but my aim would be different from my aim today. Today I am giving a lecture to ordinary Christian leaders like yourselves who want to understand more about their faith. I want my lecture to help the students to understand what the death of Jesus means for them personally. I hope they will go away thinking, 'Yes, that lecture helped me to know more clearly what Jesus has done for me by dying on the cross.'

"I will probably think and pray about this for a couple of days. Perhaps when I am going for a walk, or have half an hour to spare, I ask myself, 'What does God want me to say?' I also want to keep to a guiding principle of my life. What I say must be based on the Bible and particularly the New Testament and

the words of Jesus. Eventually I settle on two aims. These are:
1. To explain why Jesus had to die on the cross.
2. To illustrate the meaning of two verses from the Gospels:

(a) Jesus' words, 'The Son of Man came to give his life a ransom for many.' (Mark 10,45)
What does 'ransom' mean?

(b) The words of John the Baptist, 'Behold the Lamb of God.' (John 1,29)
In what way was Jesus the 'lamb of God'?

"Next, I must consider how much time I have for my lecture. Most lectures last for one hour. So allow five minutes for people to arrive and settle down. Then allow ten minutes at the end for questions, which leaves forty-five minutes for the actual lecture. That is a good length of time, as many people cannot concentrate for longer.

"I want to go on now to give the outline of the lecture and to show how I bring in these different points. I start the lecture by greeting people warmly and smiling at them. Remember that your congregation have given up their time to come and hear you. They are, in a sense, your clients. Many will be eager to hear what you have to say. So make them welcome.

"Then I tell them briefly the points I am going to consider in the lecture - that is, the two aims I mentioned. I also tell them that at the end of the lecture there will be a short time for questions.

"The next step, and a very important one, is to get the people's attention. Remember what we said about a good introduction. I do this by introducing a very simple visual aid and by telling a story. You could use a present day story, but I have decided to use the story of the call of Isaiah, described in Chapter Six of the Book of Isaiah. I will tell this story as vividly as I can, asking the people to imagine themselves in the temple with Isaiah. But before that, I show them my visual aid."

Matthew went to the side of the room and brought out two branches from a tree, lashed together to form a simple cross. He placed this against the wall where everyone could see it and paused for a moment.

"Then I would say something like this: 'Why did Jesus have to die on the cross? What is at the heart of the problem? Well, very simply, it is the problem of evil. I am going to tell you a story from book of the prophet Isaiah which many of you will know well.'

"I will then read the story from Isaiah and continue with these words: 'I want you to imagine you are in the Temple with the prophet. You have a vision of God seated on a throne and surrounded by angels and archangels. The angels are crying, 'Holy, holy, holy is the Lord Almighty.' You are terrified. You cry out with Isaiah, 'Woe is me, I am ruined! For I am a man with unclean lips and I live among a people of unclean lips, and my eyes have seen the King, the Lord Almighty.'

"Have you ever imagined what it must be like to meet God face to face? To meet someone who is utterly holy, completely pure, completely loving? And as you look on him, you realise how sinful you are. You cannot stand in the presence of this Holy God shining with an unbearable light. Evil separates us from God. And if we are cut off from God, then we are cut off from life itself. We die, die forever, for God is the source of all life. Something has to be done about the evil which separates us from our loving Father before we can come into his presence. Some will say, 'But surely God can just forgive us.' But that doesn't do away with the evil. Think how many times you remember and dwell on past sins or mistakes.

"Even though you know you have been forgiven, they don't seem to go away. Such sins have got to die, to be done away with. Jesus took this evil we have done, and the evil of the world, on himself so that when he died, the evil died with him.'"

As Matthew said this, he held up the cross. Then he continued, speaking to his six students, "Now I come to the more difficult part of the lecture. I want to try and describe the cost of breaking down this barrier between ourselves and God and explain a little of how it works. Because the subject is so difficult, I am going to do this by telling more stories. The three stories I have chosen are, first, ransoming slaves so that they are set free. This will show the cost of dealing with evil and explain Jesus' words about 'a ransom for many'. The second is the story of the Passover Lamb from the book of Exodus. This helps to explain John the Baptist's words, 'Behold the Lamb of God.' It also shows how the blood of Jesus saves us from death, the death which comes from being separated from God. The third is the story of the scapegoat in the book of Leviticus. This story helps to show how the death of Jesus actually works. I will tell two of these stories in a straightforward way, but one, the Passover story, I will tell in a dramatic way. I hope this will hold the attention of the people as I give the lecture. The first story will go something like this:

"In the time of Jesus, the Romans had many slaves. In fact, a large number of the first Christians were slaves. Just imagine for a moment that you are a slave. You work for a master who controls your life completely. You have no money. You have no clothes of your own. You have to do exactly what he tells you: clean up the toilets, clean the house, or perhaps work all day in the hot sun, digging the ground. You may have a cruel master who, if he is not pleased with your work, beats you. You have to be up and ready for work as soon as it is light and you work all day for nothing. You have no rights at all. You have no hope. If you try to escape and are caught, you will be branded on your forehead with a red hot brand or even crucified. One day, a person comes and talks with your master. He pays your master a large sum of money and then comes to you. 'Come with me,' he says, 'You are a free man now. You are free to do whatever you like, to go wherever you like.' This stranger has ransomed you; he has paid the cost of rescuing you from slavery.

"Jesus said, 'The Son of Man did not come to be served, but to serve, and to give his life as a ransom for many.' In other words, Jesus has paid the price to set us free. We can stand in the presence of God with our heads held high. We can be with

God face to face. But the cost for Jesus is dying on a cross.

"Now for the next two stories. Again, they come from the Old Testament. They are separate stories but are connected in Chapter Fifty-three of the book of Isaiah. This chapter is about the suffering servant of God. Verse seven of the chapter says that the servant of God 'was led like a lamb to the slaughter'. So the first of the two stories is about a lamb and comes from the time when the people of Israel, the Jews, were slaves in the land of Egypt. You may remember that God called Moses to rescue his people. The King, Pharaoh, would not let the people go. Because Pharaoh would not let the people go, the Egyptians suffered many plagues. And the last terrible plague was when all the first-born sons of the Egyptians died. But the Jews escaped the plague. They were told to kill a lamb and smear the blood on the doorposts of their houses. When the Angel of Death came to kill the first-born, the Angel 'passed over' the houses of those smeared with the blood of the lamb. So the first-born of the Jews did not die. They were saved by the blood of the Lamb. In a similar way, we are saved from the death which comes from being separated from God by the blood of Jesus, the Lamb of God. That is why John the Baptist, when he sees Jesus, says, 'There is the Lamb of God.'

"At this point, I need to explain why Isaiah is so important. I point out that Jesus knew the writings of the prophet Isaiah, probably by heart. He would have learnt them when he was a boy going to the synagogue. And it is certain that he saw his death as a fulfilment of the prophecy about the servant of God who was led like a lamb to the slaughter. But Isaiah also writes this about the servant of God, 'the Lord has laid on him the iniquity of us all' (verse 6). When Isaiah writes these words he is thinking about another story from the Old Testament.

"The story comes from Leviticus, Chapter Sixteen verses 20-22. Once a year, on the Day of Atonement, two goats were chosen. One of the goats was sacrificed to God. Then the High Priest, dressed in priestly robes, would lay his hands on the other goat and confess all the sins, the wickedness and rebellion, of the people. He put these sins onto the goat's head. The goat would then be led away into the desert and let go. In the time of Jesus, the goat was thrown over a cliff to die. And all those sins died with it.

"Just as the High priest transferred the sins of the people onto the goat, so God laid on Jesus the sins of the whole world. Jesus, who as I said, would have known that passage by heart, applied it to himself. He knew that God's will for him was to take on himself the evil of all the world so that, as he dies, the evil dies too. Or, as the letter of Peter says, 'He himself bore our sins in his body on the tree.'

"What does that mean for us? It simply means that we can put all the wrongs we have done onto the shoulders of Jesus on the cross. And, as Jesus dies, the sins die with him. They are wiped out forever. God deals with the power of evil by taking it on himself.

"So, if you are burdened by any kind of sin, if you feel guilty about anything you have done which is wrong or by things you have not done which you should have done, think of yourself putting those things on the shoulders of Jesus on the cross and letting them die with him.

"Now," said Matthew to the group, "I want to make this real for those who are listening so I will tell two modern stories about people who have found what I have said to be true. You may know some stories yourself which you can use. I can think of a few. One is of a murderer in prison sentenced to be executed. Through the prayers of a prison visitor, he suddenly found he was forgiven all he had done. Jesus came to him and filled his heart with great joy. He went to his death thanking and praising God that he was free from all the bad things he had done. The second is about a man who had suffered great pain early his life. That pain was still with him and really affected the way he felt. During a time of prayer, he had a vision of Christ taking onto himself all that pain, so that he was free of it.

"I have now to end the lecture in a way that will sum up

what I have been trying to teach and also in a way that will turn people's hearts to God. I think the best way of doing this is to read part of the passage about the suffering servant from Isaiah Chapter Fifty-three, perhaps selecting the verses so the reading is not too long. And before the lecture I would pray to the Holy Spirit that the meaning of the passage may sink deeply into the hearts of those listening. I will practise reading the passage so that I read it as well as I possibly can. So the passage will help those listening, and also be an act of worship to God for sending Jesus to suffer for us. I think this would make a good ending to the lecture."

Matthew opened his Bible and read the words of the prophet Isaiah,

"He was despised and rejected by men,
a man of sorrows, and familiar with suffering.
Surely he took up our infirmities
and carried our sorrows,
He was pierced for our transgressions,
he was crushed for our iniquities;
the punishment that brought us peace was upon him,
and by his wounds we are healed.
We all, like sheep, have gone astray,
each of us has turned to his own way;
and the Lord has laid on him
the iniquity of us all."

There was a short silence as Matthew ended his lecture.

Then Solomon spoke, "Thank you for that. It's given me a lot to think about."

"Right," said Matthew, bringing them back to the lesson, "now for the assessment: one good point and one bad point or something hard to understand."

"I thought the points about speaking clearly and planning the lecture were very good," said Ayung. "But some of the things you said about the cross were hard to understand."

"I liked the way you told stories," said Theresa. "They helped to keep us interested. I understood how much it cost

Jesus, but am still not sure how it works."

"I agree with you," said Margaret, "It is a mystery. But it does work in practice. I remember when I did something that was really wrong, I went into the church. I put what I had done onto the cross of Jesus. I came out feeling much better knowing I had been forgiven."

"I was interested in the story of Isaiah's vision and his sense of unworthiness in the presence of God," said Solomon. "I once knew a man who wanted to find out more about God. I told him to go away and spend five minutes each day thinking about God and to do this for a month. At the end of the month, he came back and said, 'God has spoken to me. I was terrified!' He didn't tell me what God had said, but he did become a very faithful Christian."

"Thank you," said Matthew, "but what about the bad points in the lecture?"

"You didn't talk about the devil," said Nancy. "Surely an important part of the crucifixion is overcoming the power of Satan."

"That's true," replied Matthew. "I believe very much in a power of evil. Jesus spoke about Satan a number of times. But I think that would have to be the subject of another lesson. I felt it was too big a subject to include in the lecture I have just given."

"You talked about paying a ransom in order to free a slave," said Ayung. "But surely Jesus didn't pay anyone. Did he pay God the price of setting us free?"

"No," said Matthew. "I think Jesus used the phrase 'a ransom for many' to show that setting us free was very costly. Dealing with evil had a price, and that price was the crucifixion. And when you think what that meant for Jesus, it is truly amazing.

"First, Jesus had to suffer one of the cruellest deaths there is. And added to the physical pain was the pain of taking upon himself all the evil of the world. We just can't imagine what that must have been like. It meant for Jesus being separated from God, from life itself.

"Think of his cry from the cross, 'My God, My God why have you forsaken me.' It shows how much Jesus must have loved us, to go through all that."

Solomon came in with a very surprising comment. "You know how much I like lecturing as a teaching method. But while you were talking, I really missed the discussions we have had. Is it possible to have any discussion in a lecture?"

"A long time ago," said Matthew, "I was at a Bible study where one hundred and fifty people were present. The leader started by telling two or three jokes which had us all laughing. Then he read the passage from St. Mark's Gospel about the healing of the paralysed man, where four friends let the man down through the roof.

"He then asked us to form small groups, two people next to each other with two people in the row in front. He asked us to discuss which of the people we would have been if we had actually been at the house in the story. Would we have been a member of the crowd, a Pharisee, one of the four helpers, one of the twelve, and so on? Then after about five minutes, he stopped the discussion and went around the room asking people in different parts of it who they would have been.

"I well remember one of the people shouting, 'It's alright for you people and it's wonderful to see the rabbi healing a man, but it's my house! Who's going to help me repair my roof?'

"He then went on to draw lessons from the story, bringing in each of the characters we had chosen. You can introduce discussion into a lecture, but you must make sure that the audience is in a good humour so they are not embarrassed to talk to each other."

"I felt it was just too deep for me," said Dominic, "There were things I could understand, especially the story about the goat. But I still don't understand how the lamb takes away evil."

"I wonder how I could explain why Jesus died to the

women in my group. Even though you told stories, it would have to be a much simpler talk," said Theresa. "I think for a group like mine you would have to tell more stories about how Jesus dying on the cross has helped people today."

This seemed to be the main point of criticism and Nancy summed up what they all felt when she said, "You have given us a lot to think about. Perhaps we had better go home and do that."

"I do have a question," said Dominic. "It's not a criticism of the lecture, but something I would like to know. My question is why there is so much suffering in the world. There are earthquakes and famines and people have all kinds of illnesses, some of them very hard to bear. Then there are wars, cruel dictators and terrorist groups. Why does God let people suffer? Just think of the mother in Theresa's class who lost her two babies. Couldn't God have stopped that?"

"It's one of the hardest questions in the world to answer," replied Matthew. "Many people have tried to find an answer but it is still a mystery. A long time ago I thought very deeply about this. I was quite angry with God and kept asking the question, 'Why, God, did you make a world in which there is so much suffering?'

"As I was praying, it seemed as though God was speaking. It was like a voice in my mind. And God was saying to me, 'You are angry with me? You are right to be angry. But, my child, it was the only way I could create a world which is free to develop as it chooses. I couldn't make the world in any other way. When I created the world, I knew it would not be a fair world. I knew there would be suffering. I knew there would be pain and death. If you ask, 'Why don't you stop the wars and oppression?' The only answer I can give is 'How can I stop these things without taking away freedom from the people I have created? If I stop the soldier firing his gun, or planting a mine, I make him into a puppet, forced to do my will. I want my people to be free. I want the whole world to be free. But the cost of being free is suffering for many. And the only thing

I could do was to come myself in Jesus to be with you, and to suffer with you. I shared your suffering. And every time someone suffers, I suffer because I am in them.'

"'But there is more,' said God, 'I knew there would be anger in the world because of the way it is created. So, just as you can put all your sins and failings on me, if you are angry, put your anger on me. Join in with those who hammered the nails into my hands. I willingly take your anger on myself so that it dies with me on the cross.

'And there is more again. When you die and enter my glory, when you see the glory that is in store for you, then you will see that all the suffering and pain are utterly worthwhile. Because of the death of my Son, the suffering will be turned into great joy, just as there was joy when he rose from the dead. Trust me for the great glory that is to come for you and the whole world.'"

Matthew then continued, "This isn't part of what God said to me but it came as I was thinking about what God said. Saint Paul writes, 'I consider that our present sufferings are not worth comparing with the glory that will be revealed in us.'

"I do trust God. I have seen in my own life and in the lives of others enough of the power of God to have no doubt that He is with us. And His promise that there is glory to come, glory beyond what we can ever imagine, is true. I'm afraid, Dominic, that does not answer your question, but it may help you to understand a little more."

"Help!" said Theresa. "You've given us a huge amount to think about. My head's aching! I did understand you when you said that the world has got to be free to develop in its own way and that means evil can come in. But can we have something simpler in the next lesson?"

Lessons to learn from this chapter

1. Giving a good lecture is never easy and needs careful preparation.

2. Remember to speak clearly so everyone can hear. If you use visual aids, make sure they work, but it is best to keep things simple.

3. Be clear in your aims.

4. Use stories to hold the interest of those listening.

5. Don't go on too long as people can only concentrate for a certain length of time (this applies to sermons as well!)

6. Don't give easy answers to the problem of suffering (e.g. 'it's the will of God' when it clearly isn't.) Try, with prayer, to work out your own answers.

NOTE: The outline of the lecture on The Atonement is difficult to read and understand - as is the passage about suffering. If the lecture described was given to an actual audience, it would be easier to follow because the speaker could use different tones of voice and different gestures as he spoke.

Chapter 18

Assessing lessons and the progress of students

Matthew began his lesson by summing up the different topics the group had covered during the last few weeks.

"I'm afraid we are coming to the end of the course," he said.

"Oh no!" said Dominic. "I am really enjoying this. I don't want it to end."

"How many more classes do we have?" asked Nancy.

"Just four more sessions," replied Matthew. "So I thought it would be helpful to look at the work we have covered to date. To save time, I have printed this out on a sheet. On the left, I have put the topic in simple terms. On the right I have put what I call the 'jargon'; the special terms used in adult education to describe the topic. I've also put in the topics we are going to think about this week and next week. The last two sessions are going to be lessons from you."

They looked at the hand-out he gave to each of them:

Planning a lesson	Lesson Planning
Different ways of teaching	Teaching Methods
Different ways adults learn	Learning Styles
The task of the teacher	The teacher's role
Equipment to help your teaching	Teaching Aids
Working with small groups	Group Dynamics
Different kinds of learning	Learning Domains
How to give a good lecture	Lecturing

Last two sessions
Have your students passed?	Assessment
Are my lessons any good?	Evaluation
Planning a course of lessons	Schemes of Work

"We've covered a lot of ground," remarked Ayung. "I hadn't realised how much until you showed us this summary."

"Remember," said Matthew, "that this course is very practical. I haven't said much about theory of learning. I haven't said anything about how Adult Education is developing. The course is simply designed to help you become more effective teachers. I hope that you will enjoy your teaching more. Now for today's session, I have planned this."

Matthew turned his blackboard around.

Dominic laughed when he saw that Matthew had drawn a picture of him with a worried look on his face, asking, "Will I pass the exam?" It was a question that he had been bothering about for the last two weeks. Somehow Matthew must have sensed he was worried.

Matthew noticed him laughing.

"Don't worry, Dominic," he said. "I can assure you that you have passed. But there are two pictures and I am going to combine two subjects in this lesson. They are connected, as you will see. The first is, 'How can you tell if your students have passed the course?' In other words, 'How do you assess your students?' The second subject is, 'How do I know if my teaching has been successful?' In other words, 'How do I evaluate my lessons?'"

Matthew wrote on the blackboard:

ASSESSMENT
EVALUATION

"To complicate things a bit more," continued Matthew, "each of these subjects can be divided into two headings. Let's take assessment first. Margaret and Solomon, you are teaching groups that have to pass the course to get a certificate. And the usual method of assessment is to set an examination. If the students get a certain mark, they pass. If they don't, they fail. But the rest of you teach very informal groups who are simply wanting to learn more. There's no pass or fail at the end of the course. At the same time, you do need to know if your students are learning what you teach them. So you need some sort of assessment.

"I couldn't set my students examinations or tests," said Theresa. "They would all leave if I tried! I have to be very gentle with them. However, three of them liked learning so much that they have enrolled for courses with qualifications and have come back to me for help."

"It's the same with me," said Dominic. "The men simply want to learn how to be good Christians. I do hope some will eventually become teachers of others but that is very much in the future."

"So how can we assess the progress of these students?" asked Matthew.

"It's easy for me," said Theresa. "They have to learn to write letters, then their names. Then they learn how to write words and sentences. I can check the work from their writing books. But for Dominic it is more difficult."

"I think," said Dominic, "the best way is to encourage discussion about a topic. We had a very good discussion about prayer the other day and many spoke about how they prayed and their difficulties they had trying to pray. This showed that they had taken my teaching to heart."

"Another way," said Nancy, "is to get the students to teach the class. I sent out members of my class in pairs to do some visiting after I gave a lesson about what to say. At the next lesson, I asked each pair to tell the others the good things that had happened and the problems they faced. This showed how much they had learnt and also helped me to plan the next two lessons."

"I have managed to do something similar with one of my groups," said Ayung. "I gave a lesson on leading prayers and then asked two of the group to plan the prayers for the next time. They did well."

"How about," said Matthew, "setting a simple quiz? Most people love quizzes. And you could divide your group into two and see which side wins. The questions would be based on what you have taught during the last three or four lessons.

"But now, let's look at an easier question. How do you assess students who have to pass a course? I want you to divide into pairs and write down as many ways as you can think of for assessing progress."

This time, Dominic made quite sure he was paired with Theresa. Solomon and Margaret were busy scribbling away while Nancy watched them.

"It's not fair," she said to Ayung, "they're going to do much better than us."

"Does it matter?" said Ayung. "We're not in a competition."

"I don't know about that," replied Nancy. "I think Matthew has given us this exercise to assess us and see how good we are."

"I hadn't thought of that," said Ayung. "But that's one good way of assessing students. Let's put it down."

He wrote down, 'Setting an exercise'.

He went on, "Then there's the lesson of Dominic and Theresa. Watching us teaching is a good way of finding out if we have learnt anything. We can put that down as a way of assessment."

"I think Matthew is right when he says we shouldn't rely completely on examinations," said Nancy. "But examinations are the usual way of testing students."

Ayung went on, "I suppose a teacher can tell how well the class are doing by the questions they ask and the discussions they have."

"If you remember, we did a bit of assessment when we decided on one good thing and one criticism in the teaching practice," Nancy contributed. "Matthew asked us to do the same for his lesson."

"I think that was both assessment and evaluation," Ayung replied. "Matthew was trying to find out if his own lesson had been successful."

"We also had to show our lesson plans when we did a mini-lesson," said Nancy. "So we can put down 'checking lesson plans'."

Just then Matthew interrupted, "Time's up. Let's hear what you have put down. We'll do the same as we have done before. Each group shout out one thing until we've got everything you have written down."

He made up the following list:

Watching us teach: the group to note the good and bad points of a lesson.
Questionnaires.
Setting Exercises, some to do at home.
Setting Essays.
Assignments (e.g. working out lesson plans).
Noting how students take part in discussions.
Examinations.

To Nancy's surprise, Solomon and Margaret had only got as many as she and Ayung had. Dominic and Theresa ran out of ideas before them but no one seemed to mind.

"That's very encouraging," said Matthew. "And I am interested to see that you have thought of ways which we haven't used in our course, such as setting essays and examinations. There are three other ways of assessing students, one of which I much prefer to setting an examination. Can you think of one of those ways?"

"I think the most important way," said Solomon, "would be to come and watch us teaching our own little groups. You could, perhaps, come twice, once near the beginning of the course and once near the end. That would show very clearly if we had improved our teaching."

"Yes," said Dominic. "You could tell pretty quickly if we had learnt anything from the course."

"And if we were putting into practice what we had learnt," added Nancy.

"Excellent," said Matthew. "That is a very powerful way of assessing a student. The other two ways I had in mind are: first, ask each student to keep a diary of the lessons. The diaries would be handed in towards the end of the course and I would mark them. The second is more difficult but I think could take the place of an examination. It is to ask each student to write a dissertation. For example, ask a person who is training to become a minister to write an essay of two thousand words. A good subject for someone studying to be a minister would be 'how would you apply the principles of adult education to preaching a sermon?' The student would have to apply what he or she has learnt to an important part of their future work. So I can write down four more ways of assessing a student, the last will be the subject of the next lesson."

Matthew turned back to the board and added the following points:

Students keep a diary of lessons.
Observe students teaching their own groups of people.
Set a study project - a written assignment of 2,000 words.
Draw up a scheme of work or course of lessons.

"Forgive me for asking," said Solomon, "but why haven't you come to observe us when we are teaching? I know you couldn't have visited Ayung, but perhaps you could have arranged for him to do a little local teaching and observed him that way."

"That's an important question," said Matthew. "I said at the beginning that this course was experimental. I had no budget and have done most of the preparation in my own time. When I discussed the course with the Principal of the College, I offered to teach this course because I hoped passionately that it would lead to a course on Adult Education which would be part of the college curriculum. I think that is going to happen but cannot be sure at the moment. If a fully recognised course is established, then the college will give me a proper amount of time and some money for equipment and expenses."

"Does that mean that because the course is experimental, we will not get a qualification?" asked Nancy.

"Of course you will. And your qualification will be recognised," replied Matthew. "This college has a very good reputation. If you get a certificate from the college, all organisations will respect it. You have helped to build up a course and the college will give you a qualification for doing that."

"Excuse me," said Margaret, "what would you have done if one of us hadn't been a good student; hadn't been 'up to standard', so to speak?"

"That's a good point," said Matthew. "There are two answers. The first is that we selected you very carefully. There were ten names put forward for this course. The Principal and I chose you because we were pretty sure you would turn out to be very good teachers of adults. As I said, the course is an experiment so we needed students we could rely on.

"The second is that if, after three lessons, I thought one of you couldn't succeed, I would have had a long talk with you and perhaps persuaded you that the course wasn't suitable."

"Surely some people fail courses," said Solomon.

"Yes," replied Matthew. "But a good teacher can usually tell after two or three lessons if a student is not going to be successful. The teacher can help that person by giving extra lessons. Or the teacher can suggest they take an easier or different course. In that way they don't lose face. Now let's go back to the second main question, that is, evaluation. As I said, this has two parts. It is just as important for me and also for you, to find out how good a lesson is and also how good the whole course is. We need to know how we can improve our lessons. We need to know what we should change in our courses. So what will help me to evaluate a particular lesson?"

"I think all the things you have listed are a test of the teacher as well as the student," suggested Theresa.

"You've got it," said Matthew, "even an examination. If half the students fail an exam, then either the teacher is a bad teacher or the examiners have set a poor examination. You can find out if it is a bad examination by comparing results with other colleges which have the same examination. So setting the students some work or a project and seeing if they can do it is a good test for the teacher as well as the student.

"Another simple way of evaluating a lesson is to ask the questions, 'What did you like best?' and 'What did you like least?' But never ask 'Do you understand that?' At least, not until you know your pupils well and can trust them to give an honest answer."

"If you were Chinese," said Nancy, "you would always say 'yes, I understand that' even if you didn't understand! To say 'no' would be an insult to the teacher and also you would lose face."

"It's the same with Africans," said Dominic. "It would not be polite to the teacher to say to him, 'I don't understand.'"

"You're right again," said Matthew. "Ask more subtle questions like: 'Which part of the lesson did you like least? Which part did you enjoy most?' and, perhaps, 'Which part did you find hardest to understand?' Think of questions which show whether the student has understood what you have taught. But, as I said, never ask that question directly until you have gained the full trust of your students.

"When we get to the end of the course, I am going to give you a questionnaire to fill in. And I am going to trust you to be completely honest. If you found a lesson hard, say so. It will help me to plan a better course next year. That is the best way of evaluating a course."

"That's all very well," said Theresa, "but we're back with the old problem. Half my students can't read!"

"In that case," said Matthew, "you have to ask them to be honest with you and ask the questions yourself so they answer verbally. You could, perhaps, tick off their answers on a form so you yourself have a written record. This is not easy as students may not want to give honest answers in case they offend you. But a simple question and answer could give you an idea of how successful you were as a teacher."

"Do you think we could make the list simpler?" asked Ayung. "I mean, I can't set examinations or essays. Even setting exercises might be hard."

"That's a good point," replied Matthew. "Let's see if we can make the list more practical."

He turned the board round again and made a new heading:

Simple ways of evaluating your lesson

1. Ask indirect questions about the lesson.
2.   After each lesson, give students the chance to ask questions.
3. Give the students a questionnaire (oral if people can't read) but make it fun. For example, have a quiz.
4. Observe students at work on things they have planned themselves - have they taken to heart your teaching?

"Is that better?" asked Matthew.

"Much better," answered Theresa. "All this business of assessment and evaluation is very confusing. But I can use most of the ideas on the blackboard."

"Don't worry if you don't understand the 'technical words'

or the 'jargon' as we call it," replied Matthew. "It's all about what goes on in the minds of your students. And it's about changing methods that are not very successful. I think we have discussed the topic enough, especially after last week's long lesson. Next week, we will consider briefly how to plan a course of lessons. After that, Margaret and Ayung are giving us a teaching session and then Solomon and Nancy. Now let's spend some time praying."

Before they left Matthew's house, Solomon had a word with Theresa.

"I have spoken to some members of my congregation," he said, "and they would like to help you. Two of them have some influence with the Government. Also there are a doctor and nurse who would be willing to have a free clinic in the area once a month. Do you think you could let a small group come and meet some of your people?"

Theresa hesitated. She was not sure what effect a group of well-dressed rich people would have on her community. The people were very suspicious of social workers.

On the other hand, she had been praying for a clinic, especially for the children, for months. It seemed too good an opportunity to miss.

Solomon sensed her hesitation. "I know you are thinking of 'do-gooders'," he said. "I know some people want to interfere and think they know all the answers. I've got some of those in my congregation. But the people I have spoken to really do want to help. And I think they will receive a great deal from your people as well as giving a little help. Could we try a meeting and see how it goes?"

Theresa said, "You're right. We have had our hopes raised by people who want to do good and then have disappeared after a few weeks. But we certainly could have a meeting. I will arrange that with some of my women. Please make sure your people are willing to listen to them without being offended. They will say exactly what they think."

"Good," said Solomon. "Let's fix a time."

Lessons to learn from this chapter

1. A student needs to know if he has completed the course successfully.
    This is called **assessment.**

2. Some methods of assessment are:
    a. Set simple exercises for students to do.
    b. Observe how students take part in discussions.
    c. Give the group the chance to ask questions.
    d. Set students work to do or plan at home (assignments).
    e. Get students to keep diaries of the lessons.
    f. Set examinations if appropriate.
    g. Observe students teaching, preaching, etc.
    h. Give each student a study project.

3. A teacher needs to know if their lessons have been understood and how much the students have learnt from what he/she has taught them.
    This is called **evaluation.**

4. Evaluation helps the teacher to improve their lessons. A good teacher is always trying to find better ways to teach.

5. Methods of evaluation and assessing are very similar.

6. Some simple methods of evaluation are:
    a. Ask indirect questions about the lesson.
    b. Give students (when they know each other) the chance to ask questions. Think about the questions they ask.
    c. Questionnaire (oral if people can't read).
    d. Observe students at work on things they have planned themselves - have they taken to heart your teaching?

      e.   Plan a quiz - one side of the class against the other.

7. Beware of asking students if they have understood. Most will say 'yes' even if they have not!

NOTE: Appendix I contains two examples of questionnaires.

Chapter 19

Planning a course of lessons

There was an 'end of term' feeling about the class as they met in Matthew's house for the next session. After Ruth had served them with cold drinks, Matthew began.

"This will be the last session that I take. Then we will have the two teaching sessions. The first will be from Solomon and Nancy and the second from Margaret and Ayung. Have you decided on your topics yet?"

"We've decided to do a lesson about Baptism which would suit both our classes," replied Ayung.

"We are going to look at a very difficult problem to do with Christianity and traditional religions," said Solomon. "It is a very practical problem. We are going to try and plan a lesson around the question, 'What ceremonies or projects can a Christian take part in with people who are not Christians?' We haven't planned the lesson yet, but we're working on it."

"That's fine," replied Matthew. "I will look forward to your lessons. Now for today's topic. I can't say that it is as interesting as your lessons will be but it is an important one. It is about planning a series of lessons. The technical term for the plan of a series of lessons is 'a scheme of work'."

Mathew turned to his blackboard and wrote up the title.

PLANNING A COURSE OF LESSONS
A SCHEME OF WORK

"If you are giving just one lesson, then you don't need a scheme of work. But if you are giving a course of lessons, then you need to plan what you will be teaching in each lesson. All of you, except perhaps Ayung, have schemes of work for the groups you teach. These are provided by your church or Diocese. But when you become more experienced as teachers, then you will be involved in planning courses of lessons. So we are going to think about how draw up a plan for a course."

Ayung interrupted, "I do have a course of lessons produced by my Diocese. But it was drawn up very hastily and I am not sure if it is very good. It's just a set of notes."

"In that case," said Matthew, "try teaching it for two or three months. Then discuss the scheme with the people who drew it up. Let them know the difficulties and suggest how it could be improved. Maybe what we learn today will help you to do that. Dominic, you teach from a manual which your church has given you. Can you tell us some of the lessons you have to teach?"

"Well," said Dominic, "I start by teaching the class what it means to give your life to Jesus Christ for the first time. Then I go on to talk about 'How to pray', 'How to read the Bible', 'The work of the Holy Spirit', 'What church services are about', 'The meaning of the Lord's Supper', and many more things. The first part of the course is very practical and after about three months I start teaching about what a Christian believes about God and Jesus and the Holy Spirit. My course lasts for a year and the converts meet every week except for two breaks."

"Right," said Matthew, "we could make this into a table which would go something like this..."

He turned the blackboard round and drew a grid.

Lesson	Date	Topic
1.	Jan. 12	Giving your life to Jesus
2.	Jan. 19	How to pray
3.	Jan. 26	How to read the Bible
4.	Feb. 2	Why come to church/chapel

"I could go on with all the other topics Dominic mentioned. This would be a very simple scheme of work. It has to be simple because I can't get any more detail on the blackboard!"

They all laughed. All of them were quite happy with what Matthew was saying. As Matthew had said, they all had schemes of work for their groups.

"Now," said Matthew, "I am going to make it a bit more complicated. Before you even draw up a scheme of work, you need to be able to answer the question 'What is the Aim of the course?' Just as you need an aim for each individual lesson, you need to have an aim for a whole course. There could, of course, be more than one aim but I would not advise having more than three."

"Excuse me," said Nancy, "but why is it important to have an aim?"

"An aim helps you to keep to the subject you want to teach. You ask yourself frequently, 'Does this lesson help to achieve my overall aim?' If it does not, then you change the lesson or cut it out altogether. For example, Dominic's aim could be: **To help each person to live a full and rewarding Christian life.**

"Then each individual lesson would deal with some part of

living a Christian life. To live a Christian life you need to be able to pray. You need to read the Bible and so on. Each of the lessons helps to fulfil the overall aim of the course.

"Now, I am going to ask you to do an exercise. I want you to split into two groups. Ayung, Nancy and Dominic, make one group, please. Margaret, Theresa and Solomon make the other.

"The task of the first group is to produce a scheme of work for a short course on the New Testament. The course has six sessions, each about an hour and a half long. You are teaching people who do not know anything about the Bible. Here is some paper to make notes, and a large piece of paper. When you have finished, you can write your scheme of work on the large piece so we can all read it clearly. You have twenty minutes to discuss the course and make notes. Then I will give you another ten minutes to write it up."

Matthew handed out some papers to the first group. The large sheet of paper was divided into rows and columns.

Course: Introduction to the New Testament

Group: 10 students, all new Christians, with little or no knowledge of the Bible
Course Aims:

Lesson	Topic	Aim	Notes
1.			
2.			
3.			
4.			
5.			
6.			

"The column headed 'Notes' is for you to write down any explanation or visual aids which might help in planning the actual lessons," added Matthew.

Matthew then handed the other group a similar chart.

"Your task," he said, "is to plan a short course on 'How to lead worship'. I've chosen this topic because it might help Ayung when he is training groups of villagers to take services. You may not need all six lessons but see how you go."

There was a shuffling around of chairs as they got into the two groups. Ayung was chosen to make notes for the first group and Margaret for the second. Dominic was a bit annoyed that he wasn't in the same group as Theresa but found it a change to work with different people.

Almost at the start, there seemed to be a heated argument in the first group. Matthew could hear Nancy's voice getting louder and louder. Then things quietened down and the group seemed to settle down to work together. After twenty minutes, Matthew announced, "Ten minutes to go!"

There were cries of protest from both groups.

"We need more time!" said Theresa.

"Alright," said Matthew, who knew twenty minutes was a bit short, "but only five minutes extra. Write down your results even if you are not sure you've got the best plan."

This forced them to write down what they had been discussing and by the end of the thirty-five minutes both groups had finished their charts.

The chart of Solomon, Nancy and Dominic:

Course: An introduction to the New Testament
Group: 10 students - all new Christians

Course Aims:
1. To describe and explain the contents of the New Testament.
2. To show that the New Testament can inspire and guide anyone. God speaks to us through the Bible.
Note: We must start where people are. None of them will know much about the Bible so we ask them what they know about Jesus and then tell them that the Bible teaches us what Jesus is like and what he came to do.

Lesson	Topic	Aim	Notes
1.	Members of the group to introduce themselves		
	The Bible	To show that the Bible has two parts:	Bibles needed
	Old Testament	(a) O.T. is before Jesus and preparing the way	
	New Testament	(b) N.T. is about Jesus and has Gospels, Acts, Letters, Revelation	
2.	The Gospels	(a) To introduce the Gospels and show they present different pictures of Jesus	What does 'Gospel' mean?

Lesson	Topic	Aim	Notes
	Study one Gospel story, e.g. Good Samaritan	(b) To show God teaches through Gospel stories	Picture of story
3.	The Acts of the Apostles	(a) to summarise what Acts is about	Beginning of Church
	Story, e.g. St. Paul's conversion	(b) to show how God changes lives and can change our lives	Picture of Paul
4.	The Letters	(a) To show N.T. contains many letters written by different people	Show some present day letters
	Study 1 Corinthian Ch. 13 about love	(b) what was written then can help us today	Put your name in the place of the word 'love'

	Topic	Aim	Notes
5.	Revelation	(a) introduce the book and explain why it was written	Visions of the future
	Use the words of the Book to praise God.	(b) join in the worship of Heaven.	e.g. Chapter 5 with brief explanation
Lesson	**Topic**	**Aim**	**Notes**
6.	The inspiration of N.T. 2 Timothy 3,15	(a) To teach what N.T. says about itself.	
	A meditation, possibly Stilling of the Storm	(b) To give God the opportunity to speak to us through the N.T.	

Matthew let the group study the chart for a few minutes and then congratulated those who had created it.

"This is really good," he said, "especially since it was done in such a short time. It usually takes at least half a day to plan even a short course. But I noticed there was a bit of a disagreement at the beginning. What was that about?"

Ayung said, "We had some problems at the start as we couldn't agree about the nature of the New Testament. Nancy thought it was very much written by God through the actual writers; Matthew, Mark and so on. I thought that the writers were certainly inspired by the Holy Spirit, but were still ordinary people writing down as best they could what they knew about Jesus."

"So," said Nancy, "we decided that we would base our scheme of work on things we did agree about. We all agreed that we should explain what was in the New Testament. And we all agreed that God speaks to us through the New Testament. And we agreed that the Bible, especially the New Testament, does change people's lives."

"We decided," said Dominic, "to teach the actual facts, who wrote the different books and what they were about. But at the same time include Bible studies to show God does speak to us through what they wrote."

"The other thing," said Ayung, "is that we remembered how important it is to build on what people know. So we thought it would be right to ask them what they knew about Jesus and then go on to say how much more they can learn through the New Testament. We put this in a note at the beginning."

"What do you mean," asked Theresa, "by the words 'put your name in the place of love' in section 4?"

Nancy answered, "St. Paul writes, 'Love is patient, love is kind and envies no one, is never boastful, or conceited or rude', and so on. When I read that, I put my name in place of the word 'love'. I say to myself, 'Nancy is patient, Nancy is kind and envies no one. Nancy is never boastful or conceited or rude.' It's not true, of course! But if I really want to love, then I have to try to be like that. It makes the meaning of the verses much clearer to me personally."

"That makes the words quite a challenge," said Theresa. "I am not sure I am very patient! And the one about 'keeping no record of wrongs'. If I put my name there, 'Theresa keeps no record of wrongs'. I'm afraid I still feel angry with my father and am keeping a score of the wrongs he did to me. Somehow, I've got to really forgive him! It makes you think!"

"It does," said Matthew. "We all tend to remember wrongs that others have done to us but somehow, with the grace of Jesus, we have to let such things go. But now we need to look at the second chart. Could you put your chart on the floor?"

They all gathered round and read the second scheme of work.

Course: Planning and Leading worship

Group: 10 people chosen by members of the local church
Aims: 1. 'What is worship?' To help group find some answers to this question.
    2. To show how to plan a service
    3. To enable members of the group to take a part in leading, reading etc.
Objectives: The group to plan and conduct a service for the church.
    Those taking part to speak clearly.

Lesson	Topic	Aim	Notes
1.	What is worship?	To show worship is being with God inspired by the Holy Spirit. To discuss the 5 parts of worship: Praise, listening, praying, confessing, teaching	Does the worship have a set structure?
2.	Choosing the theme	To show how to choose a theme: (a) If set lessons (b) If leader plans service.	Even with a set plan leave room for the inspiration of the Holy Spirit

Lesson	Topic	Aim	Notes
3.	Choosing the music	To teach principles for choosing hymns, songs and music. To emphasise importance of praise.	Some denominations have a set number of hymns, others allow for spontaneity.
4.	Reading lessons and leading prayers	To demonstrate and practise how to read and pray in public.	Important to be heard Prayers for healing

Lesson	Topic	Aim	Notes
5.	Teaching	To introduce principles of preaching a sermon and how to listen. To discuss other forms of instruction.	Some churches very strict about who preaches
6.	Conduct a Service	Group to plan and lead a Sunday service. Obtain feedback from congregation.	Get honest comments

"That's a very comprehensive course," said Matthew. "But can you explain some of the points you have made, especially in the notes section?"

Margaret spoke up for her group.

"When we started to plan this course, we thought it would be a simple matter. We didn't think we could find enough material for six sessions. But as we discussed it, we realised just how important the subject was.

"We felt that 'worship' is the most important thing a church or individual Christian can do. So it is very important that each person plays their part as well as they possibly can. However, the chart itself doesn't bring out the most important element and that is prayer to the Holy Spirit. Unless worship is inspired by the Holy Spirit it is an empty thing.

"The other main point is that not all churches have a structured form of worship. Catholics, Anglicans and to some extent Methodists have a set form of service but some have entirely free worship where anyone can take part at any time. Some churches have set lessons, while others leave it to the leader to choose the theme and readings. On the whole, we have planned a course for those churches which have a set form of worship."

"You know," said Theresa, "we forgot one very important thing. The first group started by finding out what people already knew and built on that. The people we are trying to teach already have a lot of experience of worship, some good and some bad. For example, I can think of very inspiring sermons and some long and boring sermons! We should really start by asking people what they think about the services of worship they go to and then go on to teach them the kind of things we've put down in the chart."

"That's a very good point," said Matthew. "But remember, you only had twenty minutes to draw up the scheme."

"You have put in the notes, 'Prayers for healing'," said Ayung. "What do you mean by that?"

Solomon answered this question. "Churches are different," he said. "In many churches, healing is a natural part of the service. People are invited to come for laying-on of hands, or sick people are prayed for by those around them in the congregation. In other churches, people are simply prayed for by name by the person who is leading the prayers. We thought that we should have a discussion about this in the lesson about prayer."

"There is one very important point," said Theresa. "I have brought this up before. Most of these schemes of work are for people who can read fairly well. What can we do about people who are not good readers or who can't read at all?"

"Your question illustrates two very important principles of Adult Education," said Matthew. "The first is that you must know roughly what standard your group is. This is technically called the 'Entry Behaviour' of the students.

"Your approach for a group where half the students cannot read is different from the approach to a group of college students. That doesn't mean, of course, that the college students are cleverer than the people who can't read. But it does mean the groups are different. So an important question is 'Who are your lessons are aimed at?'

"The second point is that there are two kinds of knowledge. There is 'head' knowledge and 'heart' knowledge. The two cannot be separated entirely.

"Head knowledge is more a knowledge of facts and how things work. Heart knowledge is more a matter of feeling and instinct. For example, you know you love someone but you cannot explain in your mind what love really is. There's certainly a great deal of heart knowledge in Christianity. And it is funny that people who think they are being reasonable can be quite emotional and do get very worked up when others argue against them.

"Both schemes had a lot of head knowledge in them. So people should end the course by knowing something about the different books of the New Testament. Both schemes had heart knowledge in that they gave opportunity for people to come close to God. I think the first group with a lot of Bible studies had more heart knowledge than the second, but that is quite alright and both schemes are good.

"However, I do have two points for you to think about. The

first is that you need some follow up. You are teaching beginners in the Christian faith. So you need something to consolidate what you have taught. Often it is good to put this into a scheme of work.

"For example, you might suggest to students who can read that they use some suitable Bible study notes. Or perhaps you could organise Bible study groups, especially for those who can't read. You needn't do these yourself, of course. You might find someone in your group who could do them. Follow up is very useful, especially with a course on the Bible. So far as the course on leading worship is concerned, the follow up is simpler. The group will be leading worship so they can discuss afterwards what went very well and what could be improved.

"The second point is this. The first group put in their notes 'starting where people are'. That means building on what the students already know. A very good way of teaching practical skills like visiting, or taking worship, is to introduce the subject with a very short course. Then send them out to practise what they have learnt for, say, four weeks. After that, bring them together and ask them what good things they have experienced and what difficulties they have had. Have they been asked questions that are hard to answer? Build the rest of the course on their experience so you are answering questions they are asking.

"So, to sum up, today's lesson is only an introduction to planning schemes of work. When you have been teaching for a time, and using other people's schemes of work, you will find that you may want to try planning your own. Do remember that what you have done today is just a beginning.

"To help you in the future, I am giving you a shortened version of my scheme of work for this course of lessons. The full version is much more detailed but you can study the summary when you have some time and it may help you in planning schemes of your own. And most important, remember to be flexible. I altered my scheme when Dominic came up with the problem of a difficult student. We have covered all the ground but not exactly in the order I had planned. So your scheme is not like the law of the Medes and Persians in the book of Daniel, which can never be altered. Don't be afraid of making changes as long as they fit in with the overall aim of your course.

"I think I have said enough so I will stop. Do any of you have any questions?"

The group didn't have any, so Matthew continued.

"Next time we are going to hear from Margaret and Ayung. Now let's have our time of prayer."

Lessons to learn from this chapter

1. When you are doing a course of lessons, it is important to draw up a plan of what you are going to teach in each lesson. This is called a 'Scheme of Work'.

2. It is good to have an 'Aim'. What do you really want people to have learnt by the end of the course? This keeps your lessons on track.

3. You need to take into account the standard of your students. It is no good teaching a course that is too hard for them as they will learn very little.

4. Similarly, it is no good having a course which is too easy and does not challenge the students. They will get bored.

5. Make a table of all the lessons you want to teach. Then decide on the order of the lessons.

6. Consider some sort of follow up to your course, especially for beginners.

7. An excellent way of teaching is to use the questions students ask. If you are training students in visiting people, after a little preparation send them out to get experience, then base lessons on their discoveries and questions. Remember St. Paul built up his theology by facing practical situations.

8. Most of the courses you teach will have a scheme of work supplied by your church organisation but there will be times when you have to make up your own. As you get more proficient as a teacher, you will be able to help plan courses.

NOTE: A summary of Matthew's scheme of work for his course is shown in Appendix E.

Chapter 20

Demonstration lesson by Margaret and Ayung

Margaret and Ayung spent a long time discussing the topic for their lesson. Eventually they decided to teach something about baptism. Ayung wanted to train a small team from a church who would prepare new Christians from their village for baptism. Margaret also wanted to help her students to teach new converts about baptism.

"We'll ask our group to pretend they are living in a village in a remote part of an island. Then we'll tell them that we are going to prepare them for baptism," said Margaret.

"Have any of the villagers been baptised already or are we teaching new converts?" asked Ayung.

"Let's make it a lesson a catechist can use to teach new converts," replied Margaret. "That will get us right down to the basics. We will also have to use the simplest possible terms. We can't use any 'churchy' or 'theological' words because they won't have heard them. Now how shall we start?"

"How about making a list of all the key ideas?" replied Ayung. "Let's have a kind of brainstorm. Then we can decide what we want to put into the lesson."

So between them they made a list of all aspects of baptism they could think of. It was quite long!

Washing clean	Water
Repentance	Immersion
Jesus born in us	Signing with the cross
Change of heart and mind	Turning away from evil
Turning to Christ	A new start
River, sea, pool??	Washing on forehead
Becoming part of church	Holy Spirit given
Jesus' baptism	Peter's speech in Acts
Dying with Christ	Confession of faith
Dying to self	Promises they make

Ayung looked at the list with dismay.

"It's just too much," he said.

"Perhaps we had better look at the lesson in a different way," Margaret suggested. "What do we really want to teach the people about baptism?"

"The heart of baptism is water," replied Ayung. "Either the person goes under the water if the service is at a pool or river, or water is poured over a person's forehead. Maybe we should concentrate on what the water does to a person. Our aim for the lesson could be, 'What does being baptised actually do to you?'"

"That sounds good," said Margaret. "But as you were speaking, I had an idea. Suppose we lead the people through a 'pretend' baptism. That will show them what will happen and we can also explain the meaning as we go along."

Ayung was quite excited by this idea and so together they

planned their lesson for the group.

The next time they met at Matthew's house, they felt a little nervous. But they were confident they had an interesting lesson to teach. They started straight away by asking the other members of the group to imagine that they were villagers. They then asked them to imagine that they had decided to become Christians after listening to a catechist. The catechist had come from a neighbouring village to tell them about Jesus. None of them knew much about the Christian faith or about the church, but the catechist had taught them about Jesus. So Ayung spoke to the group as though they were new converts from a village.

"It's wonderful," he said, "that you want to become followers of Jesus. You want to become Christians. But how do you become a Christian?"

"By believing in Jesus and following him," said Nancy.

"By being baptised," Dominic added. "The catechist told us that if we wanted to be Christians, there was a service called Baptism."

"Both of you are right," replied Ayung. "So today I want to explain more about Baptism. I want to tell you about what we do at a baptism and what it means for you. But first, have any of you been to a baptism?"

Dominic was really imagining himself to be one of the villagers.

"Yes," he said. "I went to my cousin's baptism last year. It took me two days to get there. The baptism was by the sea."

"Can you tell us what happened?" asked Ayung.

"We all met on the beach," said Dominic. "Those who were baptised went out into the sea. Then the person in charge pushed their heads under the water. But I didn't quite understand why he did that."

"I'll tell you about that in a few minutes," Ayung said. "Has anyone else been to a baptism?"

"I haven't been myself," said Matthew, also pretending to be one of the villagers. "But one of my sons told me about a baptism he had been to. He said there was a lot of singing, especially when the people went into the water. This was a river, not the sea. He said that the people who were baptised seemed really happy. He asked one of the people why they had been baptised and the person replied that he wanted to follow Jesus."

"Thank you," said Ayung. "I hope that you all really want to follow Jesus. If you are not sure, then don't be baptised yet. But now I am going to ask you a very important question. Why do you want to follow Jesus? What would you like Jesus to do for you?"

This time it was Nancy who started the deep discussion that followed. She, pretending to be a villager, described how jealous she was of another woman who seemed to find life much easier. She wanted Jesus to take away the jealousy and help her to be happy. Then Solomon said that he worshipped a powerful spirit and was always giving offerings to this spirit.

"I'm afraid," he said, "that the spirit will harm my children. I want to be free, but am frightened to stop worshipping this spirit."

There followed a very moving discussion about what people really felt inside themselves and what they wanted Jesus to do about it. At first, the members of the group made up things they thought the villagers would feel. But quite soon they started talking about what they themselves would like Jesus to do for them. Nancy said that what she really wanted was to stop feeling angry about her son when he wouldn't come to church and about her husband for not supporting her more.

The discussion was so real that Ayung let it go on for a quarter of an hour before he judged it was time to move on.

"Right," he said, "perhaps in our time of prayer, we can bring these things that trouble us to Jesus. But for the time being, let's go back to our village."

He changed his tone of voice to indicate he was the catechist again. "Thank you for talking about all these things," he said. "I want you to trust that when you are baptised, Jesus will start to change you. He may help you straight away or he may do it gradually. Jesus does change our hearts and our ways of thinking. He does change our lives.

"Now I want to show you what will actually happen at the baptism service. I will also tell you some of the words you have to say. You needn't remember them as we will think about the words again. The priest will be coming in two weeks' time to take the baptism so remember that what we are doing now is not the real thing. It is only a pretend baptism. However, before we do that, Margaret is going to read out some words from the Bible. You remember that the catechist told you that the Bible is the Christians' Holy Book. It tells us about Jesus. And it tells us about the things that Jesus asked us to do. Well it was Jesus that asked us to baptise people. Just listen to these words of Jesus."

He waited while Margaret read out words from the last chapter of St. Matthew's Gospel.

"Jesus said to his followers, 'Go and make disciples of all nations, baptising them in the name of the Father and of the Son and of the Holy Spirit, and teaching them to obey everything I have commanded you.'"

"So," continued Dominic, "we baptise people because Jesus told us to do that. Have you any questions so far?"

"Excuse me," said Solomon. "It says that Jesus told those who followed him to make disciples of all nations. What does 'disciple' mean?"

"A disciple," said Ayung, "is a person who follows Jesus. And 'all nations' means simply all the countries of the world.

"Now remember that what I am going to do is a pretend baptism. Your real baptism will be in two weeks' time at the pool in the river near the school. What I am going to do will help you to understand how you will be baptised and what it means. Now I want you to imagine that this is the river."

Ayung put two pieces of rope on the floor to look like the course of a river.

He went on, "I am going to be the one who does the baptism. We call that person a priest or minister. Margaret is a

Christian and she will carry a cross. This is to remind us that Jesus died on a cross for us. The word 'Baptism' means 'to wash'. When we wash, it makes our bodies clean. When we baptise a person, it makes not just our body clean but our whole self, our mind and our spirit, clean. It washes away the bad things in our hearts."

Ayung then pointed to the place between the two ropes he had put on the floor.

"Remember," he said, "that this is the river. Margaret will stand on this side. Imagine she is standing there with a group of people from the village who are already Christians. The rest of you stand on the other side."

As they took their places, Margaret went to the side of the room and came back with a simple wooden cross, just two pieces of wood tied together.

"First of all, I want you to stand facing away from the cross. You will be asked three questions. We will practise those answers again in a week's time. The first and most important is, 'Do you turn to Christ?' Your answer is, 'I turn to Christ.' When you say, 'I turn to Christ', I want you to turn around so that you face the cross. This means that you are turning away from your former life. You are going to start a new life following Jesus. So, do you turn to Christ?"

As the group answered, "I turn to Christ," they turned around and faced the cross.

"Now," continued Ayung, "the second question is, 'Are you sorry for your sins, the bad things you have done and the good things you have failed to do?' and the third is, 'Do you turn away from evil?' Remember that means you are turning away from all spirits and demons so you never worship or pray to them again. I told you that when we talked about being a Christian.

"The next thing that happens is that I sign each one of you with the sign of the cross. This is to show that you belong to Jesus forever."

Ayung signed each one of them with the sign of the cross,

saying, "I sign you with the sign of the cross, the sign of Christ."

Then Ayung went on, "After that you must say, in front of everyone, that you do believe in God the Father, in Jesus and in the Holy Spirit. And then we come to the heart of the baptism. And the heart of baptism is being washed by water. That is why you will go down into the river.

"Before you pretend to go into the river, remember two things about water. The first is that you wash in water to make yourself clean. So your spirit, your real self, is being washed clean. The second is that you can drown in water. So in baptism, when you go under the water, you are dying to your former life. And as you come up out of the water, you are starting to live again, to live a new life with Jesus."

One by one, Ayung led them to the centre and they stooped as they pretended to go under the water.

He went on, "I baptise you in the name of the Father, and of the Son and of the Holy Spirit. Just as water washed your bodies, so now this water of baptism washes your spirit, your whole self. Think of yourself as being washed clean of all the wrong things that you have done. The bad things are washed away by the water. You are being made clean.

"Now I want you to think of yourself as drowning to your old life. Your old life has died. You have put away the past. You are going to live for Jesus. Paul says in a letter he wrote which is in the Bible, 'If any man is in Christ, he is a new creation. The old has gone and the new has come.'"

After they had all pretended to come up out of the water, Ayung continued.

"You are now starting a completely new life. You have become part of Jesus. And you join the other Christians in their task of continuing the work of Jesus."

They all took this pretend baptism very seriously.

Ayung said, "That isn't quite the end of the ceremony or service. We will end by singing some Christian songs and saying some prayers to God. But coming out of the water is the end of the baptism. So we have been through the baptism. Have you any questions?"

"It's a lot to remember," said Theresa. "I don't think I could remember the answer to the questions I will be asked. I can remember 'I turn to Christ', but not the others."

"We'll go through them again before the priest comes," said Ayung. "You needn't worry about that."

Dominic said, "I was baptised in a sort of small swimming bath that we have at our church. But a lot of people are baptised by having water poured over their heads. You didn't talk about that."

"That is a weakness of the lesson," said Ayung. "Going under the water shows very clearly what baptism does for us. If a church used a different way of baptising I would still use the same lesson to teach the meaning of baptism. I would then have to say that pouring water over a person's head does exactly the same thing. Also, where there is a great shortage of water, it has to be done that way."

There were no other questions, so Matthew took over.

"Thank you very much, Margaret and Ayung. Now we must spend some time talking about your lesson. But first, let me give you all Margaret and Ayung's lesson plan. They let me have a copy yesterday and I managed to get it copied on the college machine."

As they all looked through the lesson plan, Matthew continued.

"I want you to do as you did before. Tell us one good thing about the lesson and then give one criticism or suggestion for improvement."

Solomon said, "I very much liked the way you explained the meaning as you went through the baptism. It is difficult to explain what baptism does mean. But by saying, 'You are dying to your past way of life' as we pretended to be under the water, you made the meaning of the action clear."

"I liked the way you used very simple terms to describe what was happening," commented Nancy. "You did avoid difficult words like 'being saved' and even the word 'church'. I've got to be careful about the words I use when I try to evangelise. But I do have one question. It's not a criticism. You used very simple promises at the pretend baptism, but the promises are more complicated. Also they are different in different churches."

"I know," said Ayung. "In my own church the promises are a little different. But we thought we should make it as simple as possible and so we used a very ancient form of baptismal vows. As I said in the lesson, the villagers would learn the promises used by their own churches the week before the actual baptism."

All agreed that the lesson had been very clear.

"Alright," said Matthew. "What about criticisms?"

"What would you have done," asked Theresa, "if no one had been to a baptism and no one could describe a baptism at all?"

"We did have an alternative plan," said Ayung. "We assumed that the catechist would come with an assistant who had been baptised. So our alternative plan was for Margaret, the assistant, to describe her own baptism. But we thought it would be good to draw out of the new converts any knowledge they already had."

Why didn't you let Margaret do the baptism?" asked Dominic. "Wouldn't it have been better to have two voices?"

"We thought about that," said Ayung. "But in a village like those I visit, there would be only one teacher. So we decided that I would conduct the lesson."

"You didn't talk about the baptism of children," said Nancy. "In our church, we do baptise babies and they can't make the promises like adults."

"Again, we thought about that," said Margaret. "But we would have to have a separate lesson to teach people about the baptism of infants. And, as you know, some churches do not baptise young children. They believe that all those who are baptised must be able to make the promises themselves."

"I did note one important criticism," said Solomon. "You didn't have a conclusion to the lesson and yet you have a conclusion in your lesson plan! Wouldn't it have been better to have had something at the end to remind people of the main points?"

Ayung looked a bit confused and then suddenly laughed.

"I'm sorry," he said. "As you say, we did have a conclusion. But to be honest, I forgot all about it. I was going to go over the key points - the promises, the believing, the signing with the cross, going under the water and prayers at the end. But I completely forgot that part of the lesson!"

They all laughed.

"I don't suppose you'll forget again," said Matthew. "That's one advantage of having practise lessons. We can make mistakes here and nobody minds. And we will all make some mistakes in our teaching. But you could, in this case, have used the students to sum up. Ask each one to remember one point. For example, get Dominic to remember the promises, Solomon the meaning of going into the water, and so on. Then at the end ask the group to summarise the key points instead of you doing it for them. Are there any other criticisms you want to make?"

No one answered and then Ayung spoke.

"There is one thing that does bother me," he said. "How much do we need to explain about the Christian faith before people are baptised? On the first day of Pentecost, Peter didn't explain much about it apart from his speech. He and the disciples just baptised people and they learnt how to be Christians afterwards. I think we don't always leave enough room for the Holy Spirit to guide people. We try to give them all the answers before we start."

"I think that is a point we all need to think about carefully," said Matthew. "Many churches do have long periods of preparation before people can be baptised. But remember that the people listening to Peter would already know about baptisms. It was a fairly common practice among some of the

Jews and they would have heard about the work of John the Baptist. So some preparation is necessary. But I think you are right, Ayung, in that we try to give too much information to new converts. It is the Holy Spirit who brings the teaching of Jesus alive and the Holy Spirit comes at the time of baptism."

"I thought the Holy Spirit came through the laying-on of hands," said Solomon. "We have confirmation services in our church for that."

"I agree that in the Acts of the Apostles, laying-on of hands is one way of receiving the Holy Spirit," said Matthew. "I'd love to talk about it more but it's a whole big new topic."

No one could think of any other criticisms, so Matthew thanked Margaret and Ayung again.

"Next week," he said, "Solomon and Nancy will give the final lesson. We will finish the course the week after with a party and the Principal himself is coming to give you your certificates."

"Do you think," asked Ayung, "that you could give us another meditation? I personally found the last one you did was very helpful. I would like you to lead us in one more."

"Of course," said Matthew. "I thought it would be good to end the party with prayers and a blessing for each of you as you leave the course and go back to your tasks. I would be very happy to lead a meditation as part of the prayers.

"But it's getting late, so let's bring to God some of the concerns we expressed earlier in the lesson and ask Jesus to grant us all a new start."

Lessons to learn from this chapter

1. One way of planning a lesson is to brainstorm for ideas and then pick out essentials. You can, of course, do this on your own. If this doesn't help, think of a different approach.

2. Ayung and Margaret included three teaching methods in their lesson:
    (a) Questions and discussion.
    (b) Demonstration with the students taking part.
    (c) Team teaching.

3. Avoid any 'jargon' words like 'church', 'repentance' and 'salvation' when teaching beginners in the faith. They need to have things put in a very simple way.

4. The discussion led to personal problems being revealed. Margaret and Ayung gave time in the prayers to deal with these.

5. Allow time for questions.

6. Be prepared to listen to criticism as well as praise.

NOTE: The lesson plan (Solomon pointed out Ayung and Margaret hadn't used a conclusion) is shown in Appendix F.

Chapter 21

Demonstration lesson by Nancy and Solomon

The next week, after Matthew had served the cold drinks, Solomon started the lesson.

"I am facing a very real problem," he said, "and I would like your advice. Next Thursday, in my Parish, there is a very important local festival. It goes back for centuries, long before Christianity came here. The villagers will go in a procession to the river. There they will pray to the river god. They will ask the river god to make sure that the water does not fail them. They will take flowers and offerings of food. And the local medicine man will sacrifice a cock to the river god. They used to sacrifice other animals as well but that got too expensive so now they offer just a cock.

"My problem is that, for the first time, I have been asked to take part in the procession. I have been asked to say a prayer to the Christian God that the waters will not fail. Last year, the river nearly dried up. The villagers think if I add my prayers to theirs, this will strengthen the prayer and the river will not dry up again. So I am asking for your advice. Do I go and say a prayer?"

Nancy then took over. "What we would like you to do," she said, "is give your immediate reaction to Solomon's problem: just one or two sentences. What do you think about the situation?"

There was a pause while people thought about Solomon's problem, then Dominic spoke up.

"I used to go to these kinds of festivals when I was younger," he said. "They were great fun and everyone got drunk. But I don't go now. The elders of my church told me I should definitely not take part in pagan festivals."

"That's more than two sentences!" said Theresa. "I think that if you don't go, you are separating yourself from the people you want to help and bring to Jesus. Do you have to cut yourself off from all traditional worship?"

"I do believe that God is really concerned about the people of the village and having a good harvest. Solomon and his congregation should be praying about that. But I don't think he should go to the festival," Matthew contributed.

"Is there any way that Solomon could go but make it clear he was praying to God through Jesus Christ and not to any river god or other spirits?" suggested Margaret.

"Does the Bible give any guidance?" asked Ayung. "What does Jesus say about taking part in pagan festivals?"

Nancy continued, "Thank you for your comments. We will have a chance to discuss the problem in more detail later. We did try to come up with some answers ourselves but Solomon and I couldn't agree! That shows how hard the problem is. So far as the invitation to take part in the procession is concerned, we both think Solomon has to say no.

"A Christian cannot take part in pagan festivals. But Solomon is more tolerant than I am - he's older, you see! And he thinks there might be another possibility."

The others laughed.

Nancy continued, "What we are trying to do in this lesson is to ask you to think about the relationship between Christianity and pagan religions. How far can a Christian accept ancient practices? How many of the old traditional ways must you give up if you become a Christian? We are not trying to give answers, but simply make the issues clearer. We will leave you, as committed Christians, to decide for yourselves what you should do.

"So first, can you think of any other things, besides these festivals, where traditional religious practices clash with Christianity? The first missionaries who came here were suspicious of everything. They banned all traditional expressions of faith. But were they right?"

"Charms!" said Ayung, "I'm worried about charms that people carry. I feel they have more faith in the charms than they have in Jesus."

"I wear a charm," said Dominic, pulling out a little stone on a chain round his neck. "My mother gave it to me to protect me from spells. Do I have to throw that away?"

The others were very surprised.

"You carry a pagan charm!" said Nancy. "What do the elders think about that?"

"They don't know," said Dominic, grinning.

"Your mother gave you the charm," said Theresa, "I think you should keep it."

"I've thought of another problem," said Matthew. "A lot of people still consult witchdoctors. I know some of my students do that. If I tried to stop them, they would not trust me as their teacher. I would become 'one of the establishment' who didn't understand them. I am trying to plan a lesson which will deal with the problem. These people are going to become ministers in the church of Jesus Christ and I do think they have to commit themselves fully to Jesus."

"How about funeral rites and praying to ancestors?" said

Margaret. "I know there is a great deal of controversy about that."

"I've never understood the church's teaching about that," said Ayung. "Praying to ancestors is wrong but praying to the Saints is alright. It doesn't always make sense!"

"Do people really pray to those who have died or just pay their respects?" asked Theresa.

"It varies," said Nancy. "Many people really believe that our ancestors can protect and help us. But I think the majority have this deep feeling that they must help the departed on their way to the afterlife otherwise the ancestors will return and haunt them! Let me write down the problems we have brought up."

Nancy wrote on the board:

FESTIVALS
CHARMS
WITCHDOCTORS
FUNERAL RITES
PRAYING TO ANCESTORS

"Can you think of anything else?"

"You've got a good list there," said Ayung. "Perhaps that's enough to think about in one lesson."

"You are probably right," replied Nancy. "So let's move on. The next step is to see if we can establish any general principles about what is allowed for Christians and what is not. Someone asked, I think it was you, Ayung, if the Bible gave any guidance. Well Solomon is going to give us a short lesson on some of the Biblical teaching."

Solomon took over. "This problem is not a new one," he said. "It goes right back to the beginning of the Christian church. And it goes back to the beginning of the church in Africa as well. St. Augustine was a bishop in North Africa about sixteen hundred years ago. It is on record that a member of his congregation said, 'I visit shrines, I consult witchdoctors and diviners, but I do not forsake the church of God.' So, Matthew, we are discussing a problem that has been discussed for hundreds of years!

"But I want to take you to the Bible. The Old Testament is very emphatic about the worship of foreign Gods. There were great problems. The people were constantly forsaking God and worshipping the Baals. These were idols and local gods like the river god in my problem. The prophets were absolutely clear. You must worship the one true God. And you must not worship idols, the moon or any other false gods. Elijah had a great confrontation with the priests of Baal on Mount Carmel. It's a thrilling story. Elijah wins and orders the prophets of Baal to be killed. But I would be in deep trouble if I killed the witchdoctor as he was sacrificing the cockerel!"

"What does the New Testament say?" asked Ayung.

"I'm coming to that," replied Solomon. "First is the teaching of Jesus. He doesn't mention idols, but he does emphasise very strongly the Commandment, 'You must love the Lord your God with all your heart, with all your soul, with all your mind and with all your strength. Then, when he is tempted by the Devil in the wilderness, he says, 'You must worship the Lord your God and him alone.' He also cast out evil spirits from people who were possessed, showing that evil spirits and God cannot live together. However, Jesus worked mainly among the Jews, who only worshipped the one God. It is St. Paul who really has to face the problem.

"I want you to think about some Christians who lived in the city of Corinth, a city in Greece in Europe during the time of Jesus. To help you think about this, we've got a bit of a visual aid."

Nancy produced six cardboard boxes, cut open and each with a small candle inside, and set them up at convenient places around the room. She lit the candles and Solomon continued.

"I want you to imagine that these are temples, each dedicated to some god or other. The names of the gods were Jupiter, Apollo, Aphrodite, Demeter, Diana, and so on, but the names don't matter. You could equally well use the names of gods people worship today like the river god or, perhaps, money! The Greek gods were, of course, pagan gods. And people brought sacrifices to these temples. After killing the animal, they gave a small piece to the god, usually to be burnt, some to the priests, and the rest they took home to eat. The local butchers would also bring their animals to the temple where they or the priests killed them. They offered some of the meat to the god and to the priests of the temple and took the rest away to sell.

"Christians, who wanted to eat meat, had to get it from butchers who, unless they were Jewish butchers, had offered part of the meat to a pagan god. The question was, 'Should Christians cook and eat that meat?' Furthermore, if they were invited to the house of a friend who was not a Christian, they would certainly be given meat that had been offered to an idol. Should a Christian eat it? Well, to cut a long story short, St. Paul advises two things. You can read this in his first letter to the Corinthian Christians.

"First, he says that a Christian is free to do whatever he chooses. He knows the idol is nothing, so it is alright to eat such meat. It all comes from the one God anyway. But, and there is a very big but, if someone still half believes in the power of the idol, then he should not eat the meat.

Also, if a Christian, by eating the meat, causes a weaker Christian to begin to doubt his faith, or get upset, then the stronger Christian must not eat it. The stronger Christian is not really loving his fellow Christian if he is causing them distress. St. Paul goes on to say, 'if what I eat causes my fellow Christian to fall into sin, then I will never eat meat again.'

"Well, how does that apply to us? I think we are free to join in some of these pagan practices as long as we are certain in our own hearts that the idol is nothing. For example, some animals are killed with a prayer which is not to the Christian God. It is alright to eat that meat. But if we are taking part in anything that leads a fellow Christian astray, then we must not join in.

"There is also another important fact. In the time of the

early Christian church, Christians were prepared to die for their faith. If they were asked to take part in idol worship, most of them simply refused and some were killed as a result. There is a very moving story about Bishop Polycarp, one of the early Bishops. At that time, people had to worship the Roman Emperor, Caesar. Polycarp was accused of being a Christian. The mob wanted to kill him but the Roman proconsul was so impressed with the gentle old man that he tried to persuade Polycarp simply to say 'Caesar is Lord' and to burn a pinch of incense to the statue of Caesar. Polycarp refused, saying, 'Eighty-six years have I served Christ and he never did me any wrong. How can I blaspheme my King who saved me?' So Polycarp was burned alive.

"However, not everything in traditional religion is idol worship. The first missionaries thought so and banned everything to do with traditional religion. But, for example, most Africans believe in a high God, as do people of other races. Perhaps we Christians should build on such beliefs and help them to know the high god much more clearly as the God and Father of Jesus. Paul tried to do this when he visited Athens and found an inscription 'to an unknown God'. He then told the Athenians more about the unknown god some worshipped. And a few Athenians did listen to his teaching.

"What, then, does this mean for the festivals and customs we have been thinking about?"

Solomon sat down and Nancy took over.

"Let's take three examples," she said. "I've got three questions here:

1. Should Solomon go to the river festival?
2. Should Dominic wear his charm?
3. Should a Christian minister allow mourners to burn paper money or take part in other pagan practices at a funeral?

Matthew and Theresa, you take question one. Ayung and Margaret, will you take question two? I'll join Dominic to try and answer question three. We've got twenty minutes to come up with an answer."

There was some lively discussion and at the end of the twenty minutes, Nancy brought the whole group together.

"Well, Theresa and Matthew, what have you decided?" she asked.

Theresa answered, "We don't think Solomon should take part in a pagan festival. But there are problems. The first is that all the people, including the Christians, are concerned about the river. The second is that God loves everyone, even the pagans, so we should love them too and understand their fears.

"That does not mean that we join in idol worship, but it does mean we have sympathy for them. If we cut ourselves off from them, they will think the church does not care. So we think that Solomon and the church should tell the organisers that they are sorry, but they cannot take part in their procession. But then tell them that the Christian church will pray to the God and Father of us all that the harvests will not fail. The Christian church will pray in the name of Jesus and anyone is welcome to come to the church and join in those prayers.

"However, we think there are two conditions. The first is that Solomon should discuss the problem with his Bishop and church council. We have to be loyal to our own particular church and so Solomon must have the agreement of the Bishop and members of his council. The second condition is that any decision should be explained to the whole congregation to ensure he does not offend weaker Christians.

"We don't know that this is the right answer, but that is what we think at the moment. And there is one more very important point we want to make. With these very difficult issues, we should pray for the guidance of the Holy Spirit. It may be that God has better plans. For example, should the church work together with people of other religions to get a dam built so there is a good water supply? It is important to seek God's guidance."

"Thank you," said Nancy, "that is very clear. But how do you think the villagers will react when Solomon challenges beliefs they have held for centuries? It truly is a hard question."

"I think," replied Theresa, "that Solomon and the Christian church have to make a clear stand against idol worship, but in as gentle a way as possible."

Nancy continued, "Ayung, Margaret, what are you going to advise Dominic?"

"Well," said Margaret, "we can't ask Dominic to give up something his mother gave him. Besides, we think it is an important symbol that his mother loves him and is probably praying for him, even though she did not die a Christian. Also, we are quite sure that Dominic doesn't think the charm has a power in itself. He puts his trust very much in Jesus."

"So we think Dominic should keep his charm," said Ayung. "However, we do suggest that Dominic should ask a priest or minister to bless the charm and dedicate it to Jesus. There are many examples of Christians adapting pagan practices to the Christian faith. For example, Christmas Day itself was originally an old Roman pagan festival."

"Thank you for that," said Solomon. "Now, what about the funeral rites?"

"We found that very hard," said Dominic. "These customs are such a deep part of people's lives. It also depends partly on the family circumstances. If part of the family is not Christian, they will feel very bad if old customs aren't followed. However, we are thinking about Christian funerals."

Nancy added, "We believe the most important thing at a funeral is to commend the person who has died into God's hands. Then we pray for the family and bless them. Once that has been done, nothing else will matter much. Burning paper money does not do any harm and shows that the person cares for the one who has died. And I can't see that burying small gifts with the person does any harm. I know many Christians put flowers into the grave to help them in their grief. However, if some custom opens the way for evil spirits to come in, we will have to say 'No' and have nothing to do with such customs."

Then she continued, "Let's sum up. Solomon and I wrote down five principles which might help and we've copied these out for you."

She handed out neatly-written lists, each with a little picture on: a charm, some crops, a grave, and so on.

> **1. Christians must not pray to idols or in any way worship them.**
> **2. Idols have no power. Christians put their trust in Jesus. But taking part in ceremonies may allow evil spirits to enter. And Christians do believe in evil spirits.**
> **3. If possible, get the whole church to agree on a course of action and make things as clear as you can to everyone.**
> **4. Beware of leading weaker people astray.**
> **5. Try to discover the guidance of the Holy Spirit.**

"Thank you for taking part," said Nancy. "I am afraid we have not given any definite answers to these questions. Our aim was to help you think about the issues. I hope we have done that. But I do have one more thing to do. I have here a candle which represents Jesus himself."

Nancy put a large candle on a table in the centre of the room. Quietly and carefully, she lit the candle.

"All these other religions in their time seemed very powerful. But they came to nothing. And nearly two thousand years later, our Lord Jesus still reigns in the hearts of countless millions of people. Jesus is the Light of the World. Praise the Lord!"

There was silence as Nancy put out the candles in the boxes, leaving the candle in the middle of the room burning.

Matthew spoke. "Thank you for that, Nancy and Solomon. You have given us much to think about. While the candle is burning, let's turn to our prayers."

Lessons to learn from this chapter

1. An example of a lesson on a very difficult but important subject - traditional   religion and Christianity.

2. Although some suggestions in this lesson are made to help answer the problems, the main aim is to encourage people to think about the issues. When teaching, it is sometimes right to raise questions rather than give answers.

3. Some teaching methods used are to encourage people to think. Note the 'aim' in the lesson plan.

4. The Bible is used to give guidance about the problem but not to give legal answers. It helps a Christian to find out what is God's will.

NOTE: The lesson plan is shown in Appendix G.

Chapter 22

Party Time

Theresa felt rather sad as the bus she was travelling on with Dominic slowly made its way up the hill towards the college and Matthew's house. She remembered the first time she had come this way and the accident that had almost thrown her into Dominic's arms. She looked at him now sitting beside her. A lot had happened in the last three months, she thought. She wondered how the others would react to the announcement that she and Dominic had decided to make.

When the two arrived at Matthew's house, they found Nancy and Margaret were helping Ruth to put food on the table. Talking with Matthew was an older person.

"Let me introduce you to our College Principal," said Matthew. "This is Theresa and this is Dominic."

The Principal asked them about the work they were

involved with. They found that he already understood some of the problems they were facing. Obviously, Matthew had told the Principal quite a lot about them and it was good to see how much interest he had taken. Just then Ayung and Solomon arrived and the party was complete.

Matthew began, "I thought I would outline the programme for tonight. First, and perhaps most important, the Principal will present you with your certificates. He also would like to say one or two things to you. Then, I want you to complete a form which evaluates the course. You will remember from a lesson we had a few weeks ago that evaluation means finding out how successful a course has been. It also helps to see how a course can be improved. This is very important for me as I may have to plan a course for college students. After that we'll have a break for refreshments. I do hope you will enjoy my wife's cooking. Finally we'll have a time of prayer. I have prepared a short meditation and also I would very much like us all to pray for each other before we leave. Now I will ask the College Principal to present your certificates."

Each of them was clapped as they went up to get the rather handsome certificate the college had designed. Then the Principal gave a short speech. He began by pointing out what important work they were doing with the small groups of people they were teaching. He hoped all would enjoy this work and keep it going. Finally he thanked them all for taking part.

"As Matthew has told you," he said, "this course was an experiment. If we, that is Matthew, myself and two Governors of the college, thought it was successful, we would incorporate such a course into the college syllabus. You may not know that Matthew and I have been meeting together every two weeks to discuss your progress and the effectiveness of the teaching Matthew has been giving you. I am very happy to say that I and the Governors have been very impressed. At the beginning of the new academic year, all students at the college will have to attend a basic course about how to teach adults. I regard this as being a very important addition to our college curriculum.

Most of the students at this college will become ministers or priests in their different churches. They will all have the responsibility of teaching others. You have helped to make sure that they will be able to do that particular part of their job more effectively. Thank you."

Matthew knew the Principal had decided to make the course part of the college syllabus but was delighted to hear it announced officially. His dream had been achieved. Now he had some hard work to do to get the full course running smoothly. He had also to adapt it to the needs of students who, unlike his trial group, had not much experience of teaching adults. He thanked the Principal who then left, explaining that he was sorry he could not stay for the meal as he had another meeting to attend.

Matthew gave out his questionnaires.

"Please be completely honest with your answers. Don't put down what you think I would like to hear, but what you really feel. It will be a great help to me when I plan my new course for the students of the college. I'm giving you your last time limit," he said, smiling. "We'll spend about fifteen minutes on this."

The next fifteen minutes were spent studying the questionnaire and writing down answers. When they had all finished, Matthew spoke again.

"Thank you very much. I'll wait until tomorrow to look at them, but there is just one more thing before we eat. Dominic has an announcement!"

Dominic stood up. He was feeling very nervous, just like he had felt when he first gave a lesson to the group. But this was for a different reason.

"I just want to say," he said rather breathlessly, "that I have asked Theresa to marry me and she has said 'yes'. We haven't fixed a date for the wedding, but I hope you will all be able to come."

He sat down rather abruptly next to Theresa as the group delightedly clapped the two of them. Then each person came up to congratulate them.

When Solomon came up, Theresa said, "Solomon, would you be willing to take the service? Matthew is going to act in place of my father and say the prayers but I would like you to marry us."

"I am very honoured to be asked," said Solomon. "Of course I will. I do wish you both every happiness."

Matthew then amused them by saying a short but very sincere grace:

"Good friends: Good meat.
Good Lord: Let's eat!"

After a very tasty meal, Matthew asked them to sit down.

"At the beginning, we decided to end each lesson with a time of prayer. It seems right to do the same now that we have come to the end of the course. Ayung, you asked me to lead a meditation. I have planned one which I hope will help you as teachers. But after that, I thought we should all pray together for each one of us. And I would like you to lay hands on each other. We will ask that the Holy Spirit will give each of us the power and strength to fulfil the tasks that lie ahead. We couldn't pray for each other in this way if we were a large class, but with such a small group, I think it will be alright. I will lead the prayer but if someone feels particularly moved by God to offer a prayer or perhaps a prophecy then please do so. Do you agree to this?"

They all nodded. Margaret and Solomon were just a little nervous at being prayed for themselves in this way. Solomon had received laying-on of hands at his ordination, but that was in a very formal setting. Both he and Margaret were very accustomed to praying for others, but Solomon had never had ordinary members of the congregation praying for him with laying-on of hands. Still, he felt it was right to take part. Then Matthew began his meditation.

Matthew had spent some time thinking about which passage from the Bible he would use. He wanted something that would encourage them and give them confidence. He nearly decided to use the first chapter of the book of Joshua where God says to Joshua, 'Be strong and of good courage for I am with you wherever you go.' But then he thought it would be better to use a passage about Jesus. Jesus was the master teacher. It seemed right that teachers should think about words of Jesus. So he used the passage which Margaret and Ayung had used in their lesson about baptism. The words were from St. Matthew's Gospel, the last four verses of the last chapter.

"Then the eleven disciples went to Galilee, to the mountain where Jesus had told them to go. When they saw him, they worshipped him; but some doubted. Then Jesus came to them and said, 'All authority in heaven and on earth has been given to me. Therefore go and make disciples of all nations, baptising them in the name of the Father and of the Son and of the Holy Spirit, and teaching them to obey everything I have commanded you. And surely I am with you always, to the very end of the age.'"

Matthew read this through carefully. He continued, pausing after each sentence to give them all time to use their imagination and see the scene as vividly as they could.

"First, imagine the disciples standing on that hill. Try to make a picture in your mind. When you have done that, put yourself in the picture, standing there with the disciples, Peter, James, John, Andrew and the others.

"Imagine the clear blue sky, the sun shining, the wonderful view. Feel the warmth of the sun upon you. Now you see a figure approaching but you cannot see who it is. What do you feel?

"Perhaps you feel you want to throw yourself on the ground in worship as others did. Maybe like some of the disciples, you have doubts. We all have doubts at times in our lives. The figure draws nearer and you recognise him. Think now of Jesus standing in front of you. Try to picture him smiling at you, his disciple.

"Now picture, if you can, Jesus speaking these words

directly to you: 'I have been given all authority in heaven and on earth. Go, then, to all peoples everywhere and make them my disciples: baptise them in the name of the Father, the Son and the Holy Spirit, and teach them to obey everything I have commanded you.'

"Maybe your task is not to baptise. Others may have that command in their hearts. But certainly your task is to teach. So listen to Jesus saying to you, 'Teach them to obey everything I have commanded you.'

"Jesus is commissioning you to be one of his teachers. He wants you to carry forward his work of teaching. What a privilege! As you teach, you are doing the work of Jesus!"

Matthew paused for a longer time to let the meaning of this sink into their hearts. It always filled him with great awe when he thought that he, a teacher, was actually commissioned by Jesus. He wanted to kneel down on the floor and adore Jesus and noticed that two or three others had left their chairs and were kneeling in worship. The presence of Jesus felt very real to him.

"Please, Lord," he prayed silently, "let this be so for all of us here."

Then he went on to what he felt was one of the most important sentences in the whole Bible.

"Now listen to Jesus saying to you personally," Matthew paused and then said very clearly, "'I will be with you always, to the end of time.'

"Jesus is with you, no matter what happens. This is the promise of Jesus to you, 'I will be with you always.' Hold fast to those words when you go about your daily tasks and as you teach others. Hold fast to those words when you face difficulties, dangers, or even despair. Hold fast to those words even when you fail him for he still loves you. Wherever you go, remember these words of Jesus, 'I will be with you always to the end of time.'"

Matthew stopped and let the silence continue for two or three minutes. Then he ended with a very simple prayer.

"Lord Jesus, thank you that you are with us now. Thank you for your promise that you will be with us always. Help us to remember your words no matter where we go or whatever happens to us. Thank you, Lord Jesus. Amen."

The others joined in the 'Amen' and Matthew let the silence continue for a little longer. Then he continued. "I want now," he said quietly, "to pray for each of you. I would like you all to gather round and add your prayers to mine. We'll start with you, Ayung, and go around the room in the order you are sitting."

"Excuse me," said Dominic, "but could you pray for Theresa and myself together. We're going to be working much more closely. Is that alright, Theresa?"

Theresa nodded. As a group they gathered first around Ayung, praying that the Holy Spirit would empower his ministry among the peoples in the islands and that no one would harm him as he sought to build up teams of Christians in each village. When they came to Dominic and Theresa, Matthew asked Solomon to lead the prayers for them.

At the end, Solomon said to Matthew, "Thank you for praying for us. Now we must pray for you and your wife and for your new course at the college. We pray that you will help many others as you have helped us."

They formed a little group around Matthew and his wife, Ruth. Matthew felt a great sense of freedom and exhilaration as they laid hands upon him.

"This prayer is being answered," he thought as they prayed. "Thank you Lord for letting my dream come true."

It seemed that no one wanted to leave after the prayers but they had to face reality. Solomon felt that someone would have to make a move and so was the first to go. The others went out to the bus together, leaving Margaret with Matthew and Ruth.

Matthew thought for a moment of them all. He would miss them. They had become very close friends during the last few months. He would see them again at the wedding but he must make sure he organised a reunion in a year's time. He thought of Dominic and Theresa and their forthcoming marriage. He was glad that they got on so well with Solomon and he was sure they would support each other. He would continue to meet Margaret as a colleague. In fact he had already suggested they work together to plan the course for the college students.

Ayung and Nancy were the ones most on his mind. Although Ayung had many friends in the town where he lived, he had a lonely task travelling to the villages. He really should have someone to help him. Perhaps he could write regularly to Ayung and also pray that someone could be found to be his assistant.

Then he thought of Nancy.

"I'm still worried about Nancy," said Matthew. "I felt quite a tension in her as we were praying but didn't think it right to say anything about it."

"Don't worry," said Margaret. "I'll keep an eye on her. We have become quite close and I think I can help her through the problems she feels she has with her family. You can't be involved with all your students."

"That's true," said Matthew.

Then, looking at his wife, he said, "Thank you, love, for your help. How about a trip to the Islands in a few months' time? We could meet Ayung's family and see how he is getting on. And we can have a holiday at the same time."

Lessons to learn from this chapter

1. It is important to bring a course to a satisfying end. People need to be able to celebrate the end of a good course. And if they come from different villages, they need to be able to say goodbye to each other.

2. It may help to give a certificate at the end. It gives status to those who have taken part in the course. It also makes the course important in the eyes of others. If certificates are given, invite an important person to present them.

3. Consider whether to invite friends, especially if it is a village event, to the conclusion of the course. This will also help others to know what is going on.

4. Matthew ended his course with a meditation and prayers of commissioning. For some courses, this can be very helpful. If commissioning is to take place, plan it as carefully as a lesson but not so carefully that there is no room for the Holy Spirit to act! If there are a large number on the course, divide them into groups of three and ask each group to pray among themselves.

NOTE: For Matthew's questionnaire, see Appendix H.

Appendices

A. <u>Matthew's lesson plan (ch.3)</u>

B. <u>Summary of mini-teaching lesson plans (ch.4)</u>

C. <u>Matthew's lesson plan (ch.6)</u>

D. <u>Lesson plan of Dominic and Theresa (ch.13)</u>

E. <u>Brief outline of Matthew's scheme of work (ch.19)</u>

F. <u>The lesson plan of Margaret and Ayung (ch.20)</u>

G. <u>The lesson plan of Nancy and Solomon (ch.21)</u>

H. <u>A possible questionnaire for assessing a lesson</u>

I. <u>Matthew's questionnaire for evaluating his course</u>

J. <u>Further suggestions for leading Bible study groups</u>

Appendix A

Matthew's lesson plan (Chapter 3)

Aims: 1. To introduce members of the group to each other
 2. To give an outline of the course
 3. Planning a lesson - to help the group discover four essential parts of a lesson plan.

Objectives: 1. Students will be able to list the four essential parts of a lesson plan.
 2. Students will be able to teach a short lesson using the lesson plan they have learnt.

Introduction: 1. Members of the group to introduce themselves - me to start. (10min.)
 2. Hand out a summary of the course giving chance to make comments. (5min.)
 3. Introductory prayer (5min.)
 4. Introduce theme of the lesson - 'Lesson Planning' (5min.)

Development: (10min.) Members of the group to work in pairs, brainstorm – write down anything they can think of which comes into planning a lesson. (30min.) List answers on blackboard. Sort answers and reduce to four headings:
Aim:
Introduction:
Development/main part of lesson:
Conclusion/Consolidation
Explain why the 'Aim' and 'Introduction' are important.

Conclusion:	Distribute copies of the lesson plan and give time for students to ask questions. If no one asks, explain briefly 'Times' and 'Objectives'.
Set homework - each person to prepare a mini-lesson lasting not more than 15 minutes on any topic they choose, together with a lesson plan using the four parts. (10min.)
At the next session, which will last longer than usual, each person to teach their lesson.
Visual Aids:	Sheet giving summary of course.

Appendix B

Summary of mini-teaching lesson plans
A = Aim: I = Introduction: M = Main part of Lesson: C = Conclusion

Solomon:
A: To teach three meanings of the atonement
I: Tell the story of Maximilian Kolbe who took the place of a man about to be killed in a concentration camp.
M: Describe three aspects of the atonement:
    (a) Satisfaction - St. Anselm
    (b) Substitution - Jesus died in our place - Martin Luther
    (c) God so loves the world - Abelard and his teaching about love
C: Atonement means becoming one with God and Jesus did that for us.

Dominic:
A: To show how important it is to read the Bible regularly.
I: Describe how I came to know Jesus.
M: Give talk about how important it is to read the Bible every day.
   Tell two stories about how the Bible has helped you.
C: Jesus speaks to us through the Bible, so do read it.

Ayung:
A: To show why I was asked to go to different villages to teach people how to run their churches.
I: Story of sick person who died before a priest could visit him.
M: The priest reported this to the Bishop who summoned a committee.
   Describe the discussion and decision.
C: Point out how hard it is for people who have been accustomed to the priest doing everything to change

their ways of thinking.

Theresa:
A: Group to discuss what to do about the sewer running through the housing and decide on a course of action.

I: Describe stream - dead animals, sewage and children playing in water.

M: Members of the group discuss what can be done.

C: Group to decide on a practical plan of action

Margaret:
A: To show that St. Mark, the writer of the third Gospel, was an ordinary Christian with human limitations and failings, yet was used by God to write one of the most important books in the world.

I: Tell students, "I want to introduce you to a friend whom I admire very much. My friend died a very long time ago and was called Mark."

M: Make clear this is what I believe about Mark - some scholars would disagree. Bishop Papias (?d.135AD) wrote that Mark was writer of third Gospel recording stories told by Peter. Short Gospel written in a poor community. Greek not good. Look up (i) Acts 15,37 frightened and ran home to Mother. (ii) Mark 14,51 frightened young man. (iii) Mark 16,8 explain ending of Gospel. For Mark proper reaction to resurrection is fear and awe.

C: I believe God used Mark, who lived among poor people and had little courage or no confidence in himself, to write the most important book in the world.

Nancy:
A: To show students different ways of evangelising.

I: Story of a person called David who went to a tent meeting and gave his life to Jesus.

M: Give a talk on different ways of evangelism. (i) Street testimony. (ii) Visiting but be sensitive (story of friend and husband who threatened to throw her out when she told him he would go to Hell if he didn't listen). (iii) Invite people to meals and give personal testimony. (iv) Tent meetings.

C: Only Holy Spirit can draw people to Jesus, so must pray for the Holy Spirit to guide you in what you say and to prepare hearts of those listening.

Appendix C

Matthew's lesson plan (Chapter 6)

Aim:
1. To help group discover at least 8 different teaching methods
2. To give 4 reasons why different teaching methods should be used.
3. (In view of Dominic's question) to show that students learn more through using different teaching methods.

Objectives:
1. Students will be able to identify at least 8 different teaching methods and
2. Will be able to give 4 reasons for using these.

Introduction: Explain that Dominic's question about proper teaching will be answered by asking students to assess this lesson giving two good points and two criticisms. (5min.)

Method:

(10 min.) 1. Heading on Board: Different Ways of Teaching (Different Teaching Methods)
Each person to write down as many different teaching methods as they can. If students struggle, use question/answer method.

(15 min.) List on board at least 8 and preferably 10 different methods.

(15 min.) 2. Why use different methods?
Oral Teaching giving four reasons and the answer to the question of previous week about what people remember.

(10 min.) 3. Discuss how much students have learnt by asking for criticisms of the lesson and its strengths.

Consolidation: Give hand-out.

Note: The times are for guidance only.

Appendix D

Lesson plan of Dominic and Theresa (Chapter 13)

Aim: 1. To lead a Bible study on Luke 4,14-30
2. To discover the main lessons from the passage as they apply to each individual in the group

Objectives: The group will memorise the words of Jesus

Introduction: Ask class to imagine they are members of Theresa's class
Theresa Explain context of story – synagogue
Prophet and Jewish feelings about Gentiles

Main part of Read passage dramatically using a scroll
Teaching Theresa to carry scroll and return to cupboard

Margaret Margaret to read narrative, Dominic to read words of Jesus.

Theresa Imagine the scene. Follow by:
  Discussion - which part of Jesus' reading from   Isaiah appealed to you most?
  What did you think main lesson of story?   (Answers only: no discussion.)

Conclusion: Read verses from Isaiah again and then all
Dominic repeat in order to memorise

Visual Aids Room re-arranged with table in centre and
needed cupboard at the back.
Scroll

Appendix E

Brief outline of Matthew's Scheme of Work (Chapter 19)

Title of Course: Teaching Adults - basic principles.

Aims: To help students to become more effective and understanding teachers.
To introduce students to different ways of teaching and the reasons for using them.

Objectives: Students will have the confidence to use what they learn when they are teaching groups themselves

Students: 6 students of varying backgrounds, all with some experience of teaching adults in small groups.

Lesson 1: Introductions
(a) to each other
(b) to the course
Planning Lessons - elementary principles
Discuss place of prayer for and during the course.

Lesson 2: Mini-teaching. Each student to give a short lesson on subject of their choice.
5 minutes to assess 1 good point and one bad point (strict timing).
Make notes for future assessment of progress

Lesson 3: Different ways of teaching. Introduce 8-10 different Teaching Methods
Explain briefly why different methods are

needed.

Lesson 4: Different ways of learning (Learning styles)
Use a short dull lecture to discuss conditioning of time at school - lessons, exams etc.
What makes a good teacher and dangers of bad teaching.
Need to change way of thinking about education.

Lesson 5: Teaching Aids. Introduce as many Aids as possible and demonstrate their use.
Discuss what Aids can be used in students' own situations, especially if there is no electricity.

Lesson 6: Leading small groups - 1st lesson.
Introduce the idea of Group Dynamics and phases in life of groups
NOTE: Lesson was changed to some extent in view of Dominic's problem.

Lesson 7: Leading small groups - 2nd lesson.
Problem students and how to deal with them.

Lesson 8: Sample lesson given by two students. Use this to assess progress.

Lesson 9: Learning Domains, lesson 1. Introduce the four simple kinds of learning under the heading MUDA.
Discuss appropriate teaching strategies for each domain
NOTE: End of lesson and prayers changed because of Nancy's problem.

Lesson 10: Learning Domains, lesson 2.
Focus especially on Attitudes - when to try and

change them and the best teaching methods to use.

Lesson 11: Assessment:
    (a) How to assess progress of students
    (b) How to evaluate lessons and courses

Lesson 12: Brief introduction to the planning of courses. Exercise in planning a scheme of work.

Lesson 13: Lesson by two students working together. Evaluate their lesson with one good point and one criticism from each of the other students.

Lesson 14: Lesson by remaining pair of students. Evaluation as in Lesson 13.

Lesson 15: Ending the course.
    (a) Presentation of certificates.
    (b) Meal.
    (c) Pray for each other and the work each has to do.

NOTE: A full scheme of work would have many more details.

There would be 7 or 8 columns with the headings for each lesson as follows:

Subject: Aim(s): Objectives: Teaching Methods: Resources: Assessment: and possibly Learning Domains.

In addition, there would be an evaluation at the end and, perhaps, 3 times during the course.

Appendix F

The lesson plan of Margaret and Ayung (Chapter 20)

Aim: 1. To show what happens at a Baptism Service
2. To explain the most important meanings of Baptism especially turning to Jesus, being washed clean and starting a new life.

Objectives: Converts will be able to describe a river baptism
Converts will be able to describe to others what it means to be baptised.

Introduction: Ayung to lead whole lesson apart from the reading

Group to imagine they are villagers. Have any of you been to a baptism before?
If 'yes', ask person to describe what took place.
If 'no', Margaret describes her own baptism.

Method: Ask question, "Why do you want to be baptised?" and "What do you want Jesus to do for you?"
Spend time discussing this.
Why be baptised?
Jesus' words from St. Matthew 28,16-20 **(Margaret)**
A pretend baptism for all students
Rope to form a river with Margaret, carrying cross.
The rest facing away from cross.
Key undertaking 'I turn to Christ' turn to face cross so turning away from former life. Go briefly through other commitments.
Baptism - go down into river in turn.
As go under explain to first two people:

(a) washing clean,
(b) drowning - dying to self
As come out, explain
(c) starting new life.
(d) joining Christians as members of church
Any Questions??

Conclusion: Go over key points:
   (a) Commitment - turn to Christ
   (b) Signing with cross - belonging to Jesus
   (c) Belief in God, Jesus, Holy Spirit.
   (d) Going into water - washed clean, dying to self
   – the heart of baptism
   (e) New life with Jesus, becoming a follower with others.

Visual Aids: Rough cross.
   Two pieces of rope to suggest river.

Appendix G

The lesson plan of Nancy and Solomon (Chapter 21)

Aim: To help people think about the issue of traditional religions and Christianity:
To draw up a list of principles on which to work.

Introduction: A problem facing Solomon asked to join a procession
Solomon Blessing the river, praying and sacrificing to the river god.
Discussion of problem in two groups.

Main teaching: Other conflicts between traditional
Nancy religions and Christianity.
Draw these out from students, but include:
Charms
Funerals
Consulting witchdoctors

Solomon Oral teaching from Bible – O.T. Elijah on Carmel
Jesus' teaching, early church - Polycarp
St. Paul's advice to Corinthians about eating meat sacrificed to idols.
Nancy Use visual aid showing different religions of the time - cardboard boxes with candles to illustrate idol temples.

Activity 3 questions to answer in groups of two:
Nancy Should Solomon join in the procession?
plus two other questions arising from discussion.

Handout Five principles for guidance.
and
Conclusion Act of devotion: light a candle to represent the light of Christ.
Nancy
Blow out candles in idol temples leaving the centre candle, the light of Christ, burning.

Visual Aids Boxes with small candles and headings Big Candle. Hand-out, Matches!

Appendix H

A possible questionnaire for assessing a lesson

Subject of lesson ....
Number in class ......

Please give your comments on the following:

Voice and delivery
....
....

Planning and preparation
....
....

Introduction
....
....

Main part of lesson
....
....

Consolidation
....
....

Use of illustration
....
....

Knowledge of subject
....
....

Use of visual aids

....
....

Student involvement and interest
....
....

General
....
....
....
....

Note: It can be helpful to have boxes to tick with the following headings -

    Excellent   Good   Satisfactory   Weak

But it is also necessary to have a space for comments.

Appendix I

Matthew's questionnaire for evaluating his course

For each topic listed up to the one entitled 'Ending a course', please tick one of the headings in the space opposite the comment. If you would like to write down a brief comment on any topic, please do this on the dotted lines.

Easy to understand **Needed more explanation** **Hard to understand**

Lesson planning
....
....
Teaching methods
....
....
Different ways of learning
....
....
Teaching Aids
....
....
Leading small groups
....
....
Different kinds of learning
....
....
Assessment and Evaluation
....
....
Planning courses
....
....
What makes a good teacher?

....
....
Ending a course
....
....

Please comment on the attitude of teacher, including voice and delivery
....
....
....
....

How will this course help you (if at all) with your teaching?
....
....
....
....

Are there any topics or other matters you feel you would like to have been included or taught in more detail?
....
....
....
....

What did you enjoy most about the course?
....
....
....
....

What did you like least in the course?
....
....
....
....

Appendix J

Further suggestions for leading Bible study groups

The book contains two methods for leading Bible study groups: leading a meditation (ch. 15 and 22), and acting out the story and then discussing the passage (ch. 13).

1. Meditation. This gives God the opportunity to speak to people directly by asking them to picture the scene, perhaps putting themselves in the place of one of the characters in the story. Remember that there may be some in the group who are not able to use their imaginations in this way. Ask anyone who finds it difficult to imagine the scene to concentrate instead on the words of Jesus or the words of a person in the story and think about what these words mean.

2. Acting out the story or 'dramatisation'. Try to get behind the words, to what people in the passage are likely to think or feel. Take, for the example, the story of Abraham being told to sacrifice his son Isaac. What would Abraham have felt when he realised God was asking him to kill his Son? I think that at first he would be very bewildered - "What, sacrifice my son??" and then as God's voice goes on relentlessly, "Sacrifice your son whom you love…" he would rebel. "No, No, NO! What kind of God are you to ask a father to kill his son?" And eventually, because he had served God all his life, a kind of despairing acceptance, "If that really is your will…" Then, what would Isaac feel when he realises his father is going to kill him? "You can't, Father… I'll run away… I hate your God…" And perhaps, "Do it quickly, Father," as Abraham pauses when the angel appears. It is an extremely dramatic story which can lead to deep discussion. In the same way, many of the New Testament stories can be dramatised, especially the crucifixion and resurrection.

3. A simple method of leading a group is to read the passage and then ask if anyone has any questions, anything they do not understand about the passage. Answer questions raised and then ask members of the group to pick out a verse or sentence which really speaks to them. But do not put pressure on everyone to speak as there may be shy people present.

4. A development of this method is to have a simple questionnaire. Get someone to summarise the passage in their own words. Then ask and discuss:
1. What do you think is the key verse?
2. What does this passage teach us about God, about Jesus?
3. Is there any example to follow? Is there any sin to avoid?
4. What is the main lesson for me in this passage?
5. Is there anything God is guiding me or us to do tomorrow or during the week, as a result of reading and discussing this passage?

This last question is important. God guides people in many different ways but especially through the words of the Bible. One of the clearest examples for me happened when I was planning a sermon based on the parable of the Good Samaritan. The thought came very strongly into my mind, 'You cannot preach that sermon until you have done something about it yourself.'

At that time, Idi Amin was expelling Asians from Uganda. I was living in a large house with plenty of room so I telephoned Christian Aid and offered to house some refugees – and then was able to go ahead with my sermon. Not long afterwards, a delightful family of Indians came to stay with me for eight months until they were able to join relatives who had fled to Canada.

If you have enjoyed this book, we would be very grateful if you would take the time to review it on the Amazon website. A positive review is invaluable and will be greatly appreciated by the author.

Please also visit the Heddon Publishing website to find out about our other titles: www.heddonpublishing.com

Heddon Publishing was established in 2012 and is a publishing house with a difference. We work with self-publishing authors to get their work out into the real world, by-passing the traditional slog through 'slush piles'.
Please contact us by email in the first instance to find out more: enquiries@heddonpublishing.com

Like us on Facebook and receive all our news at:
www.facebook.com/heddonpublishing

Join our mailing list by emailing:
mailinglist@heddonpublishing.com

Follow us on Twitter: @PublishHeddon

www.ingramcontent.com/pod-product-compliance
Lightning Source LLC
Chambersburg PA
CBHW021143080526
44588CB00008B/187